REACHING

FOR THE

RESURRECTION

A PASTORAL BIOETHICS

Loneliness, Aloneness, Euthanasia,
Meaning, Anorexia, Brain Death,
Conversion, and the Death and
Resurrection of Christ

Francis Etheredge

En Route Books and Media, LLC
Saint Louis, MO

⊕*ENROUTE*
Make the time

En Route Books and Media, LLC
5705 Rhodes Avenue
St. Louis, MO 63109

Cover credit: Sebastian Mahfood

ISBN-13: 978-1-956715-50-7
Library of Congress Control Number: 2022938328

Acknowledgments

Once again my thanks go to Dr. Pravin Thevathasan for enriching the Foreword with his own experience, to Dr. Sebastian Mahfood, OP, for the dialogue that leads to a satisfying expression of the work in the layout and book cover design, to Dr. Anthony Williams, for his careful proof reading of the text and to those who, like the Rev. Dr. Joseph Tham, LC, Dr. Ronda Chervin and Dr. Moira McQueen, for their early endorsements of the book and, finally, to Dr. Dr. Ralph Weimann for a very timely and helpful copy of his own, recently published book, which has proved to be a very valuable, complementary text on the subject of *The Bioethical Challenges at the End of Life*. Naturally, however, any imperfections in the presentation or the argument remain mine.

CONTENTS

BIOGRAPHY AND FOREWORD BY
DR. PRAVIN THEVATHASAN

Pravin Thevathasan is a graduate of the Royal Free Hospital Medical School in London. He specialized in psychiatry and although he has specialized still further, he has retained an interest in how Catholicism and mental health can complement each other. This led him to publish a Catholic Truth Society booklet entitled *Catholicism and Mental Health*. He is the current Editor of the

1

Catholic Medical Quarterly. He has an interest in pro-life issues and he has given various presentations at pro-life conferences, especially on abortion and mental health.

Pravin Thevathasan, MB.BS, MRPsych, MSc (Medical Ethics), Consultant Psychiatrist and Editor, Catholic Medical Quarterly, UK: http://www.cmq.org.uk/.

FOREWORD: THE HUMANIZING VALUE OF EXPERIENCE

Francis Etheredge knows from first-hand experience what loneliness is. He describes two kinds of loneliness: firstly, there is the loneliness of being alone with God. This kind of loneliness is healthy as it gives meaning to our lives. Then there is the destructive loneliness that can lead to death. As a psychiatrist, I have come across many people whose loneliness leads to mental disorders and even death. They have been unable to find meaning in their lives. As the Book of Genesis puts it: "It is not good that man should be alone." (Genesis 2:18).

Loneliness leads people to want to end their lives. The author notes that many people asking for euthanasia feel that they have become a burden on society. While there is good evidence that such people may be suffering from depression, I was interested to learn that many doctors who are involved in assisted suicide experience significant psychological distress themselves. As the author puts it, this may be "an almost involuntary reaction against the deliberate killing of a human being."

The author's reflections on loneliness have led me to reflect on so many different issues. Many years ago, I spent two hours trying to persuade a pregnant woman not to go ahead with her planned abortion. She knew that she was carrying a child. But she was determined to bring that life to an end. I asked her if there was anything that would make her change her mind. She immediately said that she would not go ahead with the abortion if her partner supported this decision. Her loneliness was leading her along a path of destruction. I also remember the pregnant woman who walked away from a violent partner in order to continue with her pregnancy rather than follow his determination to have her baby aborted. She was entering a lonely path. But there is life at the end of that path. She was so grateful when I handed her details of supportive pro-life groups. She did not know of their existence.

Rather than following a pursuit that leads to death, we are called to enter the pursuit of meaning, of life. Even if we have to "follow it through the labyrinthine paths through which the reality of life takes us." Even when we are treading paths that end seemingly nowhere. I know someone whose life has been seemingly a series of failures. But that person has a wonderful ability to reach out to other people, especially those in need. We can find meaning even in the most difficult of circumstances.

The section on anorexia nervosa is of great interest as I heard about someone who was told by a counsellor that it was "Catholic guilt" that was leading to her eating disorder. In fact, she made a good recovery and remained a practicing Catholic. It was heartening to read about a person with anorexia who felt so well supported by her Catholic parents and by nuns when she was at her lowest ebb. They never gave up on her.

The author ends his excellent discussion by noting that Christians find their ultimate meaning in the life, death, and resurrection of Christ. I am not saying that being a fully believing Christian stops a person from developing mental health conditions. But it certainly helps.

Pravin Thevathasan

WHAT IS IN A TITLE?

"Lord Jesus, as this day begins we remember that you are risen, and therefore we look to the future with confidence – Lord, lead us to the truth'[1].

Nevertheless, 'A culture of death is grounded on foundational structures of sin [being anti-life and anti-God] .... Rightly understood, [the spiritual dimension of bioethical issues] ... imply a fight against sin'[2].

Fr. Joseph Tham says, in his reflection on Job: 'Even though suffering universally touches our profoundest

---

[1] From the prayers of the Church for Morning Prayer, Week 2, Tuesday, p. [208] of *The Divine Office: I: Advent, Christmastide and Weeks 1-9 of the Year*, Collins: London, 1974.

[2] Adapted from Ralph Weimann's *Bioethical Challenges* at the *End of Life*, Brooklyn, NY: Angelico Press, 2022, p. 34. On the one hand, *The ABCQ of Conceiving Conception*, (published by En Route Books and Media, 2022) complements this book by considering the nature of human conception; but, on the other hand, Ralph Weimann's book gives a more thorough grounding to principles, the culture of life and death and the complementarity of faith and reason.

sensibilities and provokes in us a yearning for answers about our origin, purpose, and end, it is rarely a subject of interest in medical or bioethics journals. It is unfortunate that contemporary bioethics, because of historical reasons, has excluded a deeper discussion on suffering, possibly because of its secular bias (Evans, 2002; Tham, 2008)'[3].

One of the resources, then, open to Christians, particularly Catholics and Orthodox, is the sacrament of reconciliation with God and man; but, in addition, all the sacraments have their relationship to life, and to eternal life, including the sacrament of the sick. However, while it is good to consult a priest concerning the benefit of these graces, I can nevertheless speak as a layperson who has benefited from them, and the word of God, they help to reconcile us to God and to heal the injuries we have suffered[4].

---

[3] Fr. Joseph Tham, p. 2 of 18, "Communicating with Sufferers: Lessons from the Book of Job", Christian Bioethics Advance Access published March 22, 2013: *Christian Bioethics:* doi:10.1093/cb/cbt003.

[4] In view of the reality of the sacraments it is advisable to consult a priest about when to receive them and what benefits

'Regarding its etymology, bioethics derives from the Greek *bios* meaning life and *ethos* meaning ethics .... *bios* indicates the fullness of life, including a metaphysical perspective and relation to God, as well as to the concept[s] of death, soul, immortality, and eternity'[5].

Man is a *'religious being'*[6] and the wholeness of human nature.

So many people die from suicide, euthanasia, anorexia, brain death or loneliness, because of hopelessness and the inability to find their suffering meaningful, purposeful or, as it were, pointing to what needs addressing in a different way to what was thought or lived. The medical facts involved are of value to doctors and nurses, care workers, relatives and especially anybody going through

---

they can confer; cf. Weimann, *Bioethical Challenges* at the *End of Life*, pp. 68-69, 112-113, 121-122, 135, 138, 158-159, 174, 180; cf. particularly, the effect of medication on consciousness, as this might impair a person's preparation for death, pp. 159-160.

[5] From Weimann's *Bioethical Challenges* at the *End of Life*, p. 5, citing footnote 12: 'Cf. Angela Maria Cosentino, "Vita ..." in *Enciclopedia di bioetica e scienza giuridica* etc.

[6] *Catechism of the Catholic Church*, CCC, 28, 44-45.

what is unintelligible to them; however, it could be objected, why do we need to bring religion into it, especially the Christian religion? The point is not, however, that the Christian religion is brought into what is involved; rather, the point is that in view of our religious nature[7], the presence of so many diverse perceptions of God, spirituality and ritual through the diverse religions of the world, that God is already implicated as the Creator of man, male and female, (Gn 1: 26-27) and that we need to turn to the Creator to fully understand ourselves and what we are going through.

There are three answers, then, to the agonizing statement that "nobody knows what I am going through". In the first place, the sense of our experience isolating us is dramatically real; and, in a certain way, invites us to listen to this specific person's life-situation. On the one hand we each have our experience of suffering and, as we can, we can "touch" the pulse of pain in others even if it is a vigil, as with my mother, who declined, step by step with cancer until, accepting that hearing was the last sense to go, I sang the psalms quietly as it was nearly midnight and quiet on the ward, before I went home. And, although I missed the

---

[7] CCC, 28, 44-45.

moment of my mother's death the following morning by minutes, two of my sisters had read the morning psalms to her as she passed, peacefully, to the Father. On the other hand, in view of the fact that the Holy Bible is written through the lives of so many people and, particularly, opens up the suffering of Christ and His disciples, it is clear that there is a "place" for everyone in the word of God: a word that helps us to encounter Christ in whatever crisis we are in. And, as it says on the eve of His passion that Christ went out from the last supper singing (Mt 26: 30), and that a psalm helped to express what He was going through on the cross (cf. Ps 22[8]), so the psalms are there for us too, whatever we are going through.

Neither naïve science nor superseded philosophy and theology

On the one hand, there can be a naïve view of science that suggests that the only truth is empirical and, as it were, published by scientists, irrespective of whether those scientists are paid, directly or indirectly, to publish research that is clearly serving the bias of the clients who are

---

[8] Cf. Jn 19: 28,

funding it[9] – rather than the objective truth to be discovered and addressed by honest research. As a corollary of this, there is a definite distrust of religion as if it has nothing to contribute beyond a kind of emphasis on private beliefs and practices – as if there is something rational in denying that there is an understanding that the world has a reason, a *logos*, an intelligibility which transcends

---

[9] Cf. "The Abortion Industry, Like Big Tobacco Before It, Undermines Science | Opinion", John W. Fisher and James Studnicki, Charlotte Lozier Institute, 2/15/2022: https://www.newsweek.com/abortion-industry-like-big-tobacco-before-it-undermines-science-opinion-1678488. Cf. also other areas of research which indicate that, already, the law (for example in America, already supported a pro-life understanding of the 14th Amendment, and yet somehow this has been overlooked): Hadley Arkes, "On Overruling Roe", March, 2022: https://www.firstthings.com/article/2022/03/on-overruling-roe?mc_cid=229a4de18f&mc_eid=b3596fc5a6. Cf. also the travesties of justice involving Puerto Rican women who were given excessive does of hormones to "test" the side effects of what was going to be marketed as "The Pill", the obscuring of the health-value of ovulation by unnecessary use of hormones, people suffering from syphilis being kept off antibiotics which would have helped, the unborn who are treated as experimental subjects in laboratories etc. etc.

randomness, chance and unpredictability – but takes account of it all the same. In other words, there is a *logos* that leads to all kinds of radical and far-reaching accounts in a whole multitude of disciplines, from philosophy to cosmology, psychology to neuro-science, botany to medicine and beyond. Without realizing it, then, it is possible to teach, learn and research a reductionist understanding of the human being and the universe in which we live; and, therefore, as unintelligible as it is, it is possible to think that all that exists is matter and that the words we use do not express anything but the activity of particles – as if the very intelligibility of sound and electronic signals does not contradict this: that a message has a medium of transmission but the medium of transmission is not the message!

On the other hand, then, there are limitations to both philosophical and theological thought, especially when it does pertain to what is empirically observable and is clearly superseded, empirically, philosophically, and theologically,[10] as is now the case with our understanding of conception going beyond both Aristotle and St. Thomas

---

[10] Cf. *Conception: An Icon of the Beginning; Mary and Bioethics: An Exploration; The Human Person: A Bioethical Word,* and *The ABCQ of Conceiving Conception.*

Aquinas and many modern authors too - and yet, as with all good developments, the truth draws coherently on what remains perennially valid in thought and practice because what is real is really, ongoingly present today[11].

Altogether, then, it is necessary to recover a wholesome account of human nature, neither diminishing nor exaggerating what is found. Therefore, let those who reflect upon illness, in all its forms, be open to the perception of the psychosomatic whole of the human person, one in body and soul (cf. *Gaudium et Spes*, 14[12]) while, at the same time, aware of the possibility that just as sin goes beyond our reasonable recognition of what is wrong, so grace exceeds the power of evil and brings about a good beyond what we can obtain for ourselves[13].

---

[11] Cf. Etheredge, Chapter 2, *Volume I-Faithful Reason*: https://www.cambridgescholars.com/product/978-1-4438-8680-2.

[12] Documents singled out by a Latin title are either from the *Second Vatican Council*, as in this case, or a published papal document.

[13] A more specific discussion of human participation in the sufferings of Christ is to be found in "Chapter Two: Mary is the Choice of God", in *Mary and Bioethics: An Exploration*: https://enroutebooksandmedia.com/maryandbioethics/.

The unexpected relevance of an Old Testament "moment"

On the one hand, drawing up an inclusive and comprehensive account of the human person involves accepting the wide variety of human experience, of our own experience, letting us inform and verify the general characteristics that a sound anthropology proposes and develops from time immemorial[14] – expressing the profound complementarity of Christian belief, experience, empirical science and philosophy. But, on the other hand, there is also the benefit of a perception which arises out of the nature of faith itself; and, in a rather simple and marvelous way, this is well illustrated from the book of Daniel.

There is a new emperor, Cyrus of Persia, who worships a god called Bel. Daniel, however, denies that Bel is more than a lifeless statue, even though Bel appears to consume a vast quantity of food. Daniel lets the priests of Bel depart and Cyrus sets out the food, as usual, for Bel to eat. However, before Daniel and Cyrus depart and Cyrus seals the door of the temple, Daniel instructs his servants to 'bring ashes and spread them all over the temple floor,

---

[14] Cf. Etheredge, Chapter 1, *Volume I-Faithful Reason.*

with no other witness than the king' (Dn 14: 14). Then Daniel and Cyrus leave and the king seals the doors to the temple. The following morning, Cyrus enters the temple and says to Daniel, as the food has gone:

"'You are great, O Bel! There is no deception in you!" But Daniel laughed. And restraining the king from going further in he said, "Look at the floor and examine these footprints". "I can see footprints of men, of women and of children" said the king, and angrily ordered the priests to be arrested' (Dn 14: 18-21).

In other words, there is a clarity to Daniel's understanding of the statue, Bel, precisely because he knows who the true God is, having experienced His help many times. More generally, then, there is so much that is about an intelligent understanding of the universe, of human nature and of the elements, that it is clear that the biblical authors grasp reality even if, as with the opening account of creation, they use an analogy of the week[15], or of an

---

[15] Genesis, 1-2.

unfinished vessel[16], to render an understanding of their subject. Indeed, analogies are both about recognizing the limitations of human understanding and, at the same time, rendering what they do know of what is both a mystery and its visible expression.

The challenge of joy: A way forward

There are many references to personal experience in the course of this book and, quite simply, it both roots the work in the reality of a life as, in so many instances of what is described, there are so many glimpses of the tragic situation in which people really live and die; and, therefore, to communicate the pastoral nature of this book it is necessary to show that God acts, over many years, in many different, but real situations. Therefore, to conclude, I read an article recently about "Christian Joy and Human

---

[16] *Golmi*, literally meaning 'unfinished vessel', is a unique word for referring to David in the simplest moment of his beginning but, as implied, open to development (Ps. 139: 16); another translation renders it as 'my unfinished substance'; cf. *Conception: An Icon of the Beginning*, "Chapter Two: Scripture and the Beginning of Human Being", particularly pages 190-199: . https://enroutebooksandmedia.com/conception/.

Sadness"; and, as in so many situations we find ourselves, there is a temptation to give up, to be destroyed by an event, an illness, an inexplicable change in our health or circumstances:

> Thus the "Morning Prayer" of the Church comes with this announcement: "Come into the Lord's presence singing for joy."

This announcement of joy, coming together with the opening of the first psalm, "Come, ring out our joy to the Lord" (94), really comes to contradict the problems of the day and the tendency to look at myself, my sins, problems, illness, Covid caught by two of our eight children and now my wife, crises in the world and impending global conflicts. In other words, God is always calling to us to remember His love, His help and all that is good; and, in a way, it sets me aright for the day beginning with His call to be joyful, as I say, as a contradiction to how easy it is to start to complain and to worry and to fizzle like a firework and to go out![17]

In the end, then, the title *Reaching for the Resurrection* is about coming to the loving care of all who need our help, recognizing that there are limits to what we can do alone, that we need the sharpened perception that helps us to discern the needs of others and the help of the word which goes beyond us to illuminate the heart's hidden depths. But, at the same time, we are *reaching for the resurrection* because, in all humility, we are in front of human freedom and the mystery of God's dialogue with us in His word and in our prayers.

Thus the emphasis of this particular book is on the dialogue that leads to life, whether life lived fully here (cf. Jn 10: 10) or the fullness of eternal life; and, therefore, while some clarification of principle and practice has been given here, I encourage the reader to consult the more technical or comprehensive works for more about the specific characteristics of illness and treatment that pertain to the various conditions referred to in this book. At the same time,

---

[17] A response to an article by Sarah Greydanus, "Christian Joy and Human Sadness": https://www.hprweb.com/2022/01/christian-joy-and-human-sadness/#comment-217024.

however, it is necessary to raise objections to the treatment of human beings which disregards the whole person or contradicts the basic premise that life is to be lived to the end; and, therefore, only once death is established is it licit to action consent[18] to the possibility of organ donation.

---

[18] Cf. the discussion on consent in Weimann's *Bioethical Challenges* at the *End of Life*, pp. 197-210 – but also in the light of the book as a whole and the controversy surrounding whether or not "brain-death" is the death of the whole person.

CHAPTER ONE

PART I OF III: LONELINESS TO "ALONENESS"

In this first piece, a personal account of loneliness is then set in a contemporary context and differentiated from an aloneness with God.

"Modern man listens more willingly to witnesses than to teachers, and if he does listen to teachers, it is because they are witnesses"[1].

At first sight it may seem that loneliness and euthanasia, the deliberate killing of another human being at his or her request, have nothing in common; but, both because of the literature on the subject and the links between the desire to die, the problem of the meaning of human experience or its abandonment, it becomes clear that there is a common pursuit which, if neglected, leads to death: an ontological death. This ontological death of the desire to

---

[1] Cf. Blessed Paul VI, *Evangelii Nuntiandi*, 41, quoted on p. 28 (paragraph 22), of the preliminary document, *Lineamenta*: Synod of Bishops: XIII Ordinary General Assembly: The New Evangelization for the Transmission of the Christian Faith.

live, search and find the meaning of our lives is, literally, a dead end. What we need is to be set in motion: to set out, once again, on the path of life and, possibly, this will give us a purpose in what we both hope to receive and, together with what we have discovered, we will need to share with others. What, precisely, coagulates or configures for each one of us may vary; it would be impossible to imagine that it would be otherwise – but the common element is that of going towards death, *ennui*, a trial of the meaninglessness of life and discovering or being discovered that the experience is so meaningful that it must be shared.

Loneliness-in-context

At the beginning of secondary school, scarcely aware of what was required for the "11 plus exam", I went to a grammar school and began to fail. It was the practice to punish failure with a public, and sometimes private caning; and, although enduring these humiliations outwardly, I resolved not to cry and thus ensued a kind of psychological suffocation of the suffering I experienced. At fourteen, a few years later, I both ran away briefly to London and really did not know why except that I was unhappy and, around the same time, I tried to commit suicide but, in front of the possibility of meeting Jesus Christ and the apostles as judges, I was afraid and started drinking water to dilute the tablets that I had taken. At the time, I never talked about the experience of humiliation, neither did I admit that I did not understand our class-work, nor could I see the point in school; and, no matter how many times I changed classes, to begin with none of my choices made sense and I frequently abandoned the courses that I had chosen to do.

What is loneliness?

In my own experience I discovered loneliness at about sixteen, although I had suffered from it for some years in a more hidden way. I discovered loneliness living in a bed-sit in London. Having come home from gambling at college, having lost my bus fare, and therefore having had to walk home, my father said as I was not working – so why didn't I give up on my courses and get a job? Within a few hours, then, I had hitched up to London, some fifty years ago; and although I had had a sister who lived nearby, she had a boyfriend and I hardly ever saw her. So, in what did this loneliness consist?

In the first place, this was more or less my first time "out of my family" and, therefore, it was my first experience of being away from the presence of my parents and the coming and going of my brothers and sisters – I was the third of seven and four of my siblings were at home with me. Although I did not realize it until I was on my own, I was clearly undeveloped in many ways. While I had played football at home I had no knowledge of the game, neither did I follow it nor did I have friends with whom I talked about it; I simply played it. Not reading, either books or newspapers, not going to the cinema or to theatres, neither a part of any group or conscious of any interests, it was very clear to me that I was "friendless"; indeed, the very basis of friendship, of having interests or an outlook or something in common with others, was simply not present. What transpired, then, was that outside of working in an office as a very junior member of staff, I either played table tennis at work or led a very solitary existence of batting a ball against a wall near where I lived, shopping and starting to read. I had taken some picture-paints to London but I never used them.

You could say that just as an octopus depends on its suckers to anchor it to objects, so a denuded person, a person without interests, was like a "sucker-less" octopus and therefore was unable to be-in-relationship to others. In essence, then, there are many facets to being faceless and unable to enter into contact with others but the primary two, as I experienced them, is the proud denial of suffering and, therefore, the "unshareable" interiorized suffering and, more generally, the undiscovered nature of who I was, what my interests were and who I was willing to share this with.

The stripped octopus grows suckers[2]

It is particularly evident that now, some fifty years later, surrounded by a wife and eight children, numerous other people, whether neighbors, members of the Church, correspondents or people I pass in the street when

---

[2] I did not marry until I was forty and the account of the deterioration, the wandering and searching, the suffering and the redemptive word of God and the progress of family life that this change implies is in various books: Volume I-III of a trilogy: *From Truth and truth*; *The Human Person: A Bioethical Word*; *The Family on Pilgrimage: God Leads Through Dead Ends*; *The Prayerful Kiss*; *Rust and Gold*; *Within Reach of You: A Book of Prose and Prayers*, all published by En Route Books and Media over recent years etc.

delivering papers with my children, that there are so many points of contact, from simply saying "good morning", passing comments on the day to being more or less immersed in so many ongoing conversations about people's lives and interests that it is abundantly clear to me that I am no longer a smooth octopus incapable of clinging to anyone or anything. Indeed, if anything, there are now so many possibilities in a day for brief or more extended exchanges with people that it is a matter of making sure that I do some work while attending to the needs of those around me and simply sharing the brightness and beauty of a flecked pink sky, spotting a particularly able snail that has climbed several feet up into the bean plants or the discovery of growing cabbages from what is normally a discarded part of it[3].

It is particularly important to me to be "taxi-dad", to talk before bedtime and prayers with our children, heeding the advice of St. Don Bosco that this is a "providential time" to converse with them as well as to be up at breakfast to joke and talk with them before school. In other words,

---

[3] Cf. Francis Etheredge, *Prayers of An Unlikely Gardener*, forthcoming from En Route Books and Media (probably, 2022).

being aware and sensitive to my wife and children is a constant and wonderfully worthwhile ingredient of every day.

The social context of the times in which we live

There are two types of relationship, as it were, somewhat conflated under "loneliness": a loneliness leading to "aloneness" with God and a loneliness leading to death. In positive terms, then, we are created through relationship – for relationship; and, if this is radically frustrated – a desire to die manifests how profoundly our nature is orientated to being with another or an "Other".

Right from earliest times Aristotle recognised that *man is a social animal*; and, even if we wish to take exception to comparing man with an animal, except as animated by a soul, the point of the gift of relationship is nevertheless made by him. Nevertheless, the nature of man is brought out more deeply by understanding that the whole history of the modern term, person, is really derived from understanding that the being of man, based as it is on the mystery of the Blessed Trinity, is really that to be a person is to be a being-in-relationship[4]. Indeed, in *Genesis* we discover that God Himself addresses the social nature of man in terms of both the virtue, the strength, of the companionship of marriage and, by implication, the suffering of being alone: 'It is not good that the man should be alone' (Gn 2: 18).

However, this does not suppose that the only two relationships are marriage or the religious life; but, more widely, it does imply that relationships are of their nature of real love: self-giving love: 'God is love': 'Love is therefore the fundamental and innate vocation of every human being'[5].

---

[4] Cf. Cardinal Ratzinger, "Concerning the notion of person in theology": https://www.communio-icr.com/files/ Ratzinger 17-3.pdf; and cf. Francis Etheredge, *The Human Person: A Bioethical Word*: https://enroutebooksandmedia.com/ bioethical-word/.

[5] St. John Paul II, *Familiaris Consortio*, 11, but also the end of 16.

Loneliness leading to "aloneness"

If man is a 'religious being'[6], then understanding what a person experiences will depend on his or her openness to the full range of human meaning.

There is an "aloneness" with God – even if, at times, that aloneness with God requires God to dramatically sustain the person who is "alone" with Him; and, therefore, when Elijah was fleeing for his life and was ready to die, from both exhaustion and a sense of being humanly alone, God sent an angel to give him food for the journey, indeed a very Eucharistic gift: 'a cake baked on hot stones and a jar of water' – not once but twice (1 Kings, 19: 1-9): a gift, ultimately, leading to an encounter with God Himself (cf. 1 Kings, 19: 9-18).

However, this "aloneness" is of its nature a relationship and indeed may well involve the communion of saints and their intercession: St. John of the Cross, although long since dead was, through his writing, a source of strength for St. Thérèse of Lisieux 'in her deep

---

[6] *The Catechism of the Catholic Church*, 28; hereafter, *CCC*.

loneliness'[7]. Indeed, even in the difficult circumstances of her life as a contemplative nun, St. Thérèse discovered that 'her vocation was love and this embraced all vocations'[8].

At the same time, however, marriage is not exempt from this kind of loneliness or "aloneness", which is defined by an intense inability to communicate the estrangement that is taking place in a marriage when, for a variety of reasons, a person does not feel understood by his or her spouse. One of the most helpful antidotes to this is to accept that this is a human experience, even if profoundly painful, and is encompassed by Mary, the Mother of the Lord, at the foot of the cross and indeed by the Lord Himself on the cross[9]. In other words, the principal that psychological development is facilitated by sharing our personal experience goes on being necessary throughout life, whether a person is married or not.

---

[7] John O'Brien, OFM, *The Darkness Shall Be the Light*, p. 198.

[8] Ibid., p. 193.

[9] One particular weekend away with the *Neocatechumenal Way* involved the introduction of the song, "Sola a Solo", "Alone with the Alone"; and, as a part of it, we were invited to share this kind of experience.

Finally, there is a desire to die which is not pathological but is, as it were, integral to the relationship between ourselves and God and is referred to by the saints themselves. St. Martin of Tours, apparently ready to go to God, was yet moved by the 'pleading' of his brothers in religion and prayed: 'Lord, if I am still needed by your people, I will not refuse the work. Your will be done'[10]. Again, for St. Paul this desire to die was not to be rid of this life so much as to be with God (cf. Philippians, 1: 19-26). To be led, then, to a death leading to the fullness of eternal life with outstretched gratitude, as it were, and a longing to meet the *Lord of Life*, to be in the company of those who have gone before and, indeed, to be accompanied by our guardian angel as we come into the presence of the all enflaming God – is a celebration of life and not a negation of the life lived and the people with whom it has been lived!

---

[10] From "A reading from the letters of Sulpicius Severus" on the feast day of St. Martin of Tours, p. 390* of Volume III of *The Divine Office: The Liturgy of the Hours According to the Roman Rite*, published by Collins, Glasgow, Dwyer, Sydney and Talbot, Dublin, 1974.

CHAPTER TWO

PART II OF III:
LONELINESS LEADING TO EUTHANASIA

In this second piece, the relationship which leads to euthanasia expresses an inadequate anthropology of the human person.

Loneliness leading to death

'Former U.S. Surgeon General Vivek Murthy <u>says</u> the most common pathology he saw during his years of service "was not heart disease or diabetes; it was loneliness"'[1].

Carl Jung found that 'many people were afflicted with hopelessness and anxiety'[2], which he understood to be the

---

[1] Amelia Worsley, "A History of Loneliness": https://theconversation.com/a-history-of-loneliness-91542.

[2] John O'Brien, OFM, *The Darkness Shall Be the Light*, p. 84, printed in Great Britain: https://www.amazon.co.uk/ Darkness-Shall-Be-Light-Journey/dp/B09DMXTL9V/

emergence of a spiritual problem which 'coincided with the declining influence that traditional religions, most prominently Christianity, have had on Western societies over the past several centuries'[3]. Indeed, one author found that loneliness began to be a problem in the '16th Century, when it signaled the danger created by being too far from other people'[4]. As regards those who want to permit euthanasia, or even seek it themselves, there is the work of Viktor Frankl[5]. Frankl thought there were many layers where illness could arise, and that one of them was due to failure to find meaning in life'[6].

So, as we are religious by nature, what about the spiritual significance of what we suffer and the social situation in which we exist: What about the meaning of our life and our experience of loneliness in the times in which we live?

---

[3] Ibid.

[4] Amelia Worsley, "A History of Loneliness": https://theconversation.com/a-history-of-loneliness-91542.

[5] E.g., His book called: *Man's Search for Meaning.*

[6] P. 100 of a prepublication manuscript by Dr. Ronda Chervin, *The Battle for the 20th Century Mind,* viewed with permission of the author (St. Louis, MO: En Route Books and Media, 2022).

In *Gaudium et Spes*, the Church says: 'They will stand by them as children should when hardships overtake their parents and old age brings its loneliness' (48).

But what happens when the extended family shrinks to a few children, the nuclear family is uprooted from its "locale" and children, if there were any, were no longer local and are simply overwhelmed by the demands of their own lives, hours of work and the difficulties of finding time to travel or to even be-in-communication virtually, not to mention the decline of village and country side populations or the rising cost of living there because of commuter traffic? Just as isolation seemed to increase when people were housed in flats rather than on the same street, so disrupting the network of kin and neighbourliness in a society may be more significant than we realize. What about the increasing number of undiscovered deaths in Japan, to the point where there is now a commercial work of going in to remove the decayed body? More widely, too, the contraceptive and abortion mentality, even considering people a burden, worthless, lacking a quality of life, parasites or polluters of the planet all indicate that relationships have ceased to be the central human reality and that, in its place, there has arisen a kind of claim that even to live is to be a "carbon footprint" vandal, or a cost-analysis "loser" who has lost out on being kept alive as against bringing about his or her death.

To put it in terms of modern parlance, loneliness is about being "out of the loop". However, in terms of anecdotal evidence of people who have committed suicide, there was either a presence on social media or a certain "loudness" which seemed to disguise an interior reality that was completely different. When, then, a particular student committed suicide[7], even those who had known this person from childhood were shocked. In other words, the interior life of a person can be very different to the outward, either virtual or "outgoing" appearance of a person; and, therefore, this seems to indicate a kind of

---

[7] To understand the scale of the problem, 'Mohsen Naghavi [and team] concluded that there were about 817,000 suicides worldwide each year between 1990 and 2016', Weimann, *Bioethical Challenges* at the *End of Life*, p. 115, citing footnote 2: "Global, regional, and national burden of suicide mortality 1990 to 2016: systematic analysis for the Global Burden of Disease Study 2016" etc. But, even if suicide is a mortal sin, because of the possibility of diminished responsibility, the Church prays for those who have committed suicide, CCC, 2283, cited on p. 121 of Weimann, *Bioethical Challenges* at the *End of Life*.

incommunicable, interior "aloneness" – but without the sense of being in a relationship to God.

There is a kind of loneliness, then, which leads to a different kind of death – more a wilting of the very root of life, a draining of the very desire to be in communion with others and a hopelessness in front of the possibility of ever being happy. There may well be a mixture of psychological and spiritual factors involved in this type of loneliness; indeed, it could even be called a "relational deficit" of the kind in which one person is unable communicate who she or he really is: a kind of asphyxiation of interiority owing to it being, for whatever reason, un-communicated.

Loneliness, euthanasia, and the trauma of death

According to a 1980 document issued by the *Congregation for the Doctrine of the Faith*, a *Declaration on Euthanasia*, "By euthanasia is understood an action or an omission which of itself or by intention causes death, so that all suffering may in this way be eliminated. Euthanasia's terms of reference, therefore, are to be found in the intention of the will and in the methods used" (CDF, DE, II) [8].

And, it needs to be added, the deliberate killing of a human being is on the conscience of all who intend it; and, as such, is an act or omission which will, of itself, dialogue with the person in view of the principle, intrinsic to the conscience, "do good, avoid harm"[9].

If euthanasia is the deliberate killing of anyone, from the unborn to the elderly, and every stage and situation in life in between, then it is, literally, a license to kill; and, if this is the social context in which the question of suffering arises, we need a renewed understanding of the whole person and the nature and significance of human suffering and, therefore, how to help. However, there is also a time where death is occurring and, owing to the reality of the situation, while death is not being hastened, it is time to accept it:

---

[8] Cf. Weimann, *Bioethical Challenges* at the *End of Life*, p. 86; citing the widespread use of euthanasia as well as the CDF, DE, document cited.

[9] Ibid., p. 97.

'if a person is, for example, suffering from cancer in the terminal stage and it is impossible for him/her to drink and eat, then the process of dying should not be prolonged. In these cases the following principle needs to be applied: *impossibilia nemo tenetur* – nobody is committed to the impossible'[10]. However, 'an omission of ordinary care should never be the "sufficient cause" for death'[11].

Whatever, then, in the case of those seeking euthanasia, the extreme sufferings that warrant careful and well managed palliative care of the terminally, or extremely ill, there appears to be more than a superficial link between loneliness and dying by the deliberate action of another. Indeed, in a recent study, there was an explicit link between loneliness and euthanasia[12]. Not to mention, in a

---

[10] Ibid., p. 106.

[11] Ibid., p. 107.

[12] "Study Uncovers euthanasia deaths based on loneliness in the Netherlands: Source: Euthanasia Prevention Coalition": '19 of the 53 MGS euthanasia deaths listed loneliness as a primary reason': https://oneofus.eu/study-uncovers-euthanasia-deaths-based-on-loneliness-in-the-netherlands-source-euthanasia-prevention-coalition/.

different piece, a dearth of interest in referring 'suicidal patients to psychologists'[13]. Or even, in view of the power of persuading vulnerable people to opt for euthanasia, the pressure of argument; hence the following account of why a woman's husband changed his mind and shocked his wife with the request for euthanasia:

'She found out that the one nurse in palliative care had spoken to him for two hours in the middle of the night, convincing him that it was the right thing to do".[14]

---

[13] 'Right To Life UK spokesperson, Catherine Robinson, said: "In Oregon, if one doctor refuses to partake in euthanasia, the patient is generally able to "doctor shop" until they find a willing executioner. There is zero state oversight, and the system relies on self-reporting by doctors who stand to gain from the business, and rarely refer their suicidal patients to psychologists"': https://www.lifenews.com/2021/08/12/scientists-want-people-fitted-with-euthanasia-chip-that-kills-you-at-first-sign-of-dementia/.

[14] Alex Schadenberg "Is Death Becoming an Industry in Canada?": https://alexschadenberg.blogspot.com/2021/11/is-death-becoming-industry-in-canada.html.

In view of the growing prevalence of euthanasia as a response to life's experiences, there is also a negative impact on the provision of palliative care, ranging from the withdrawal of funding because of not providing euthanasia, the suffering of doctors who collaborate with euthanasia and the growing recognition that people are opting for euthanasia because it is the only option and 'are fearful of being a burden'[15].

Examining what has been found more closely, both from the point of view of the doctor administering what is not a treatment but a method of killing a person and the experience of the person being killed, there are clearly problems.

On the one hand, 'up to one half of doctors who participate in an assisted death experience significant psychological and emotional distress (9). Refusals by physicians in Canada to participate in assisted deaths are not based on religious or moral grounds, but because of the emotional burden of enacting a patient's premature death and

---

[15] "The impact of assisted dying on hospices and palliative care – Dr Claud Regnard": https://ehospice.com/editorial_posts/the-impact-of-assisted-dying-on-hospices-and-palliative-care/.

awareness of psychological repercussions on themselves and the clinical team (10)'[16]. In other words, in practice, there is a human, almost involuntary, reaction against the deliberate killing of a human being.

On the other hand, it is shocking to see that the whole process is being approached so clinically, as if assisted-dying is not morally problematic and has not already caused significant stress[17] and suffering to doctors, nurses, patients and relatives and involved a kind of euphemistic

---

[16] "The impact of assisted dying on hospices and palliative care – Dr Claud Regnard": references 9 and 10 in this excerpt are to two sources: 9 is : Kelly B, Handley T, Kissane D, et al. "An indelible mark" The response to participation in euthanasia and physician-assisted suicide among doctors: a review of research findings. Palliative and Supportive Care, 2019; 18(1): 82-8. https://doi.org/10.1017/S1478951519000518; and 10 is: Bouthillier M-E, Opatrny L. A qualitative study of physicians' conscientious objections to medical aid in dying. Palliative Medicine 33(9): 121-20.

[17] Cf. Nancy Preston, "The Conversation": "Its stressful to kill somebody" etc: https://theconversation.com/its-stressful-to-kill-somebody-the-healthcare-workers-who-support-assisted-dying-173024: One doctor who was all for euthanasia says "I can't do it anymore".

suggestion that administering death can be so clinically controlled:

'Shavelson and Parrot have identified which patients are more likely to linger, and can recommend adjustments. People with gastrointestinal cancer, for example, don't absorb the drugs as well. Former opiate users often have resistance to some of the drugs. Young people and athletes tend to have stronger hearts and can survive longer with low respiration rates'[18].

At the same time, doctors are not necessarily present, the medication they are using may be regarded as experimental and death can be unpredictably drawn out[19]. In

---

[18] "Doctors seek life-ending drugs that smooth the way for the terminally ill" by Lisa M. Krieger: https://medicalx-press.com/news/2020-09-doctors-life-ending-drugs-smooth-terminally.html; and cf. also "Is an assisted death 'quick and painless'?" by Michael Cook: https://alexschadenberg.blog-spot.com/2021/11/is-assisted-death-quick-and-painless.html.

[19] JoNel Aleccia, "Docs In Northwest tweak aid-In-dying drugs to prevent prolonged deaths": https://eu.usato-day.com/story/news/2017/02/16/kaiser-docs-northwest-

other words, what are people actually going through to bring about this kind of feedback on bringing about a person's death is far from a suffering-free death.

Clearly there are immense and important parallels between what is happening to a person who is being euthanazed and a child being killed by abortion, those who are doing it and those affected by it.

On the nature of death

'"We're learning. Hypothesis, data and confirmation. This is what science is," he said. "Our job is to stop the heart; that's what they want us to do'[20].

It is almost as if it is simply a "medical challenge" to bring about an abrupt, unnatural death that, in the process, expresses a willingness to experiment on the living – resulting, in some cases, in hours of trauma. In the brutally honest explanation of what these men are doing,

tweak-aid--dying-drugs-prevent-prolonged-deaths/98003110/.

[20] "Doctors seek life-ending drugs that smooth the way for the terminally ill" by Lisa M. Krieger.

"Our job is to stop the heart", they inadvertently raise the question of whether or not brain death is death. Indeed, if the whole intention of these men is to find a way to stop a person's heart, and by definition end that person's life, are we not in another area as well: that of the controversy surrounding "brain death" as a device for harvesting organs from the living – rather than an actual definition of death? In other words, if these men, who are specializing in bringing about death, consider stopping the heart as the crucial determinant of whether or not a person is dead, then does this not undermine the credibility of brain death as a criterion of death?

Law, however unfounded on the good of life, leads to law

At the same time, as evidence is gathered from around the world, it is not a matter of imagining, fearing to consider the possibility that the criteria for euthanasia will widen; it is the reality that once it is legally allowed to kill an innocent person, the range of who falls within that scope simply widens and widens. In Canada, after assisted suicide was illegal from 1862 to 2016, it was legalized that year and then in 2021 the access criteria were widened: euthanasia was originally granted if death was reasonably foreseeable and then 'for those whose death was not reasonably foreseeable' and then in 2023 there will be a review of the current prohibition on euthanasia for those suffering from mental illness[21]. In the context of this situation, in Quebec, an inquiry was undertaken in view of 70 year olds and over accounting for 92% of Covid-19 deaths between February and July of 2020; and, while specific deaths would need to be accounted for, an evaluation of the overall situation termed it '"massacre" by "systematic ageism"'[22]. In a tragic, specific and poignant example of this: there is the discrepancy between *not* being allowed visitors during a Covid-19 lockdown and *being allowed visitors* as she was killed[23]. What happened, then, to the

---

[21]Tabitha Marshall, "Assisted Suicide in Canada", last edited December 3rd, 2021: https://www.thecanadianencyclopedia.ca/en/article/assisted-suicide-in-canada.

[22] Alex Schadenberg, "Québec Doctor testifies that some Covid patients were euthanized rather than treated":

https://alexschadenberg.blogspot.com/2021/11/quebec-doctor-testifies-that-covid.html.

[23] Wesley J. Smith, November 26th, 2020, "Elderly Woman Euthanized to Avoid Anguish of Lockdown Loneliness": https://www.nationalreview.com/corner/elderly-woman-euthanized-to-avoid-anguish-of-lockdown-loneliness/.

simple accompaniment of this woman during her two-week lockdown that so inspired her fear of its return?[24] Were there other factors in her situation that have not come to light? Why could the family visit for her death but not previously – if only it was at the distance of being able to talk but not embrace?[25]

Therefore, as Archbishop Anthony Fisher, OP, observes, speaking from his own experience of a life-threatening condition, 30 years of pastoral care as a priest, the prevalence of Catholic Institutions providing health care and the ongoing Canadian situation[26] – there is not a risk but a social certainty of widening access to euthanasia

---

[24] Smith, "Elderly Woman Euthanized" etc.

[25] Cf. various experiences of lockdown in *Within Reach of You: A Book of Prose and Prayers*: https://enroutebooksandmedia.com/withinreachofyou/.

[26] Cf. Alex Schadenberg, "Québec committee supports euthanasia for incompetent people but not for mental illness", but yet it seems to have permitted it in principle in 2021 as 'Bill C-7, that was passed by federal parliament in March 2021, permits euthanasia for mental illness alone': https://alexschadenberg.blogspot.com/2021/12/quebec-committee-approves-euthanasia.html.

once it is legally permitted[27]. Moreover, if there is a context of "elder abuse" then there are already symptoms of social decline which both facilitate the possibility of euthanasia and indicates that the love of the elderly is already a "dying" characteristic of a modern society[28]. In other words, the very establishing of legal precedents becomes the vehicle by which there is established wider and wider access to euthanasia; and, therefore,

'it will soon be extended to the chronically sick not just the terminally ill, the mentally ill not just the physically sick, those who not sick at all just tired of life or feel they are a burden on others, not just consenting adults but the unconscious and children'[29].

---

[27] Cf. "Archbishop Anthony Fisher OP to the NSW parliamentary inquiry into euthanasia", December 17th, 2021: https://www.catholicweekly.com.au/archbishop-anthony-fisher-op-to-the-nsw-parliamentary-inquiry-into-euthanasia/.

[28] Cf. Alex Schadenberg, January 12th, 2022, "New Report On Elder Abuse In Australia: Implications For Euthanasia": https://alexschadenberg.blogspot.com/2022/01/new-report-on-elder-abuse-in-australia.html.

[29] Archbishop Anthony Fisher, OP, October 15th, 2021, "Euthanasia's devastation: bad luck for the have-nots in our

Doctor or what?

What kind of evidence counts in an 'evidence-based medicine'[30]?

What we are confronted with is an increasing mentality of disregarding the reality of what a person experiences, how a person dies, what effect drugs have, such as "home abortifacients"[31] and the widespread practices of administering harmful hormonal contraceptives, the

---

brave   new   two-class   society": https://www.catholic-weekly.com.au/euthanasias-devastation-bad-luck-for-the-have-nots-in-our-brave-new-two-class-society/.

[30] This is referred to in an article on the covid-19 vaccines, by Lucie Wilk, "Why have we doctors been silent?": https://www.conservativewoman.co.uk/why-have-we-doctors-been-silent/.

[31] Cf. "Petition by Caroline Farrow, CitizenGO <petitions-en@citizengo.org>": *"Every single month 495 women in the UK require emergency care after going through a DIY abortion at home"*: A Catholic doctor, cardiologist Dermot Kearney, who helps women who want to reverse what they have done and save the life of the child and who now needs support because he is being investigated for doing this.

actual practice of taking the life of a child in the womb, IVF procedures that join sperm and egg in a glass dish and overlook the act of God giving the gift of life as an interpersonal gift, freezing embryos, discarding[32] or experimenting upon them, surgically altering the gift of a person's sex, when there is no ambiguity, and the whole program of robbing organs, whether of the nearly dead or the imprisoned.

The original definition of a doctor is that of a teacher, an instructor, or a guide[33] and a physician is one who is trained in a 'knowledge of nature' and the 'art of healing'[34]. Indeed, St. Thomas Aquinas said that medicine, like education, is assisting a natural process – not supplanting it. There is, however, a related root to the word 'teacher'

---

[32] Among the many varieties of ministry that there are is that of burying the early remains of a child, "I can't begin to tell you how much this means to me. To know that these babies were laid to rest with so much dignity – thank you!': Sacred Heart Guardians and Shelter laura@sacredheartguardians.org: Email update, Tuesday, 16th November, 2021.

[33] "doctor": https://en.wiktionary.org/wiki/doctor.

[34] "physician": https://en.wiktionary.org/wiki/physician.

which is 'to show'[35]. All three of these concepts are accompanied by the tradition of the *Hippocratic Oath* and its relationship to the natural law maxim: do good and avoid
harm. In other words, it is perfectly consonant with the
origin, history and development of medicine that it is 'evidence based'[36] and that the learned show forth what they
have learnt about the knowledge of nature; and, just as it
is possible to see what there is 'to show', so it is possible to
point back to what is seen – so that what there is to show
is seen by others. Thus a dialogue with reality as it is must
be essential to good medicine as it is the basis on which
real progress is made. A key observation by a doctor examining my eldest son's deteriorating hands was the
"pooling of blood"; my son is a university student and
tends to sit very still when working, in a somewhat cold
house. And, subsequently, we have suggested a variety of
hand and arm exercises to stimulate the circulation in his

---

[35] Daren K. Roberts: https://www.linkedin.com/feed/up-
date/urn:li:activity:6866378446084337664/.

[36] A recovery of this evidence based work is evident in *Humanae Vitae, 50 Years Later: Embracing God's Vision for Marriage, Love, and Life*, edited by Theresa Notare, Washington,
DC: The Catholic University of America Press, 2019.

hands; but, as we found when he was at home, holding his hands upright, from time to time, was a significant help to recovering the skin from splitting and pussing.

The key word from the doctor, that has made life-changing sense, was the "pooling" of blood: that the deterioration in my son's hands and my legs could be, in addition to other factors, causative of the skin deteriorating. Thus, due to the blood not changing very effectively and, as a result, pooling and, because of pooling, an agent or agents in it attacking the skin. Therefore: A small but significant change can be lifesaving as in a leg that was going black from clots, poor return valves and varicose eczema which has, after nearly eleven months of being periodically elevated vertically, and having gone through the shedding of many layers of skin, has begun to regain its normal color – albeit it they are not completely pink as yet[37]. In other words, after twenty-five years of deterioration, which neither regular, moderate walking or cycling prevented, changing the blood in my legs by putting them

---

[37] Cf. Francis Etheredge, "Legs: On Pain and Healing" in *Within Reach of You: A Book of Prose and Prayers*: https://en-routebooksandmedia.com/withinreachofyou/.

vertically up against a wall has radically improved their color and my general wellbeing.

What is significant, however, is the "selective focus" of what constitutes evidence and, in the field of loneliness and euthanasia particularly, the poor grasp of the person as a whole: of the psychosomatic whole of being one in body and soul and "from" and "for" relationships – both to God and to each other; indeed, it could even be called a poverty of thought when it comes to an adequate anthropology and, therefore, one wonders where doctors and nurses will encounter, not just an enriched understanding of the human person – but a truly realistic account of the whole of human personhood?

The words we use: To smooth acceptance or to reveal reality

In view of all that this piece has examined concerning the deliberate killing of a person, its experimental nature and range of effects on the person being killed, on family members, others, physicians and medical staff – how our language hides the reality that we know to exist when we use the following phrases:

'such [as] "assistance in dying"; "the prescription of substances which can be orally ingested"; "prescribing and providing the means of self-administration"; and "the substance or substances may be administered"[38].

In its stark reality, how is it possible not to compare what is going on now, in medical practices throughout the world, with what went on in the death camps of the *Second World War*? Do we suppose that democracy is an infallible expression of humanity when it allows one group of people to kill another; to discriminate, in other words, against the life of those either completely innocent, suffering or under the misapprehension that dying through the hands of others is a "neutral" choice or an answer to the problem of the meaning of human experience?

---

[38] Cf. Noreen O'Carroll, January 19th, 2022, "Euphemisms mask the true nature of assisted suicide and euthanasia: *Disguising the true meaning of words is a powerful weapon in the "right to die" armoury*": she discusses the language in the Irish, Dying with Dignity Bill, 2020, https://mercatornet.com/euphemisms-mask-the-true-nature-of-assisted-suicide-and-euthanasia/76937/; but see also, St. John Paul II, *Evangelium Vitae.*

CHAPTER THREE

PART III OF III: MEANING AND WORD

In this third piece, there is a word which has the possibility of re-opening the pursuit of meaning.

In the words of Mother Teresa:

We can cure physical diseases with medicine, but the only cure for loneliness, despair, and hopelessness is love. There are many in the world who are dying for a piece of bread but there are many more dying for a little love'[1].

Here, then, it is not about what we have done to ourselves, whether through attempted suicide, the unforgiving of others or living a life unconscious of ourselves or other people – so much as being a person who is 'dying for a little love'.

---

[1] *A Simple Path: Mother Teresa by Mother Teresa:* https://www.goodreads.com/quotes/139677-the-greatest-disease-in-the-west-today-is-not-tb.

There was once a man who had lost his legs and lived, as it were, for a cigarette, who rarely spoke and exuded depression. A young man came to the house to decorate the flat in which he and wife lived and, it transpired, although this man had children, they never visited him. The young man started coming round to take the man out, either to his workshop to be with him outside, with a cigarette, or to go on bumpy walks through the lanes in his wheelchair. The older man, enlivened by these visits, began to look forward to the young man's visit and to get ready for them – even if it wasn't always possible for the young man to come; and, indeed, the older man's wife saw her husband's spirit change through these simple outings and to start to ask, "When is he coming?"

The reality of suffering: to suffer or to suffer

In this essay it has emerged, really, that either we suffer, or we suffer. Whether we are dying, lonely or simply ill, there is a suffering that we either accept or reject; but, if this suffering is rejected, it is not necessarily supplanted by suffering less – rather there is a suffering in refusing to accept suffering. The suffering entailed in euthanasia, in the whole program and process of being deliberately killed, is no less a suffering as that entailed in being lonely, ill or dying; however, what may be different is our ability to enter into what is happening: that the more preoccupied we are with avoiding what our suffering is about, with the process of not thinking it through or seeking some way of abandoning the experience – the more we deny the possibility of suffering being meaningful and we enter into a kind of pursuit of the pointlessness of it. Maybe the tragic irony of seeking death deliberately is that it becomes a deliberate denial of the meaning of life and entails, as it were, an increasing effort of denial to the point of involving others in the process of death – instead of being together in the pursuit of life.

Is this the suffering described by T. S. Eliot?

"Unreal City,
Under the brown fog of a winter dawn,
A crowd flowed over London Bridge, so many,
I had not thought death had undone so many'[2].

---

[2] This excerpt is from "The Wasteland", p. 62 of T.S. Eliot, *The Complete Poems and Plays*, London: Faber and Faber, 2004.

There may be times when we have sat in silence and we were 'uncomfortable with just sitting there and felt the few minutes to be very long. In the short few minutes many found themselves getting in touch with their own inner reality'[3]. And, while more on the impression of the opening of "The Wasteland", as a whole, John O'Brien comments: 'the earth is dead. There are no roots. There is no prospect of re-birth. There is an absence of God, an absence of meaning, an absence of purpose. Modern life doesn't present us with any prospect of resurrection. There is no hope. People are dust'[4]. Indeed, there is a kind of suffering where it 'brings about bitter, twisted person-alities, broken in themselves and inflicting further harm and brokenness on others'[5]. But Julian of Norwich 'held out hope to even these that one day they would find peace'[6].

---

[3] John O'Brien, OFM, *The Darkness Shall Be the Light*, p. 131.

[4] Ibid., p. 15.

[5] Ibid., p. 234.

[6] Ibid.

Indeed, as John O'Brien says earlier, 'With many people taking their lives we need to provide places of welcome where people can discuss their emotional issues and find acceptance'. In other words, while many of us will strive alone to make sense of our lives and fall foul, as it were, of the fallacy of solving our own problems, the reality of "walking with others", while it takes many forms, is an almost absolute necessity. For just as Aristotle recognized that we are 'social animals' so our healing is a social reality and, probably, the problems in our lives have arisen out of a rupture of many social relationships.

The alternative, then, to the pursuit of death, whether inadvertently or deliberately, is to enter the pursuit of meaning and to follow it through the labyrinthine paths through which the reality of life takes us; and, in the course of that pursuit, there will be many dead ends, diversions and insights that pebble the way and which, in retrospect, make a path visible. It could take fruitless visits to doctors, misunderstanding of the symptoms, incarceration, either in a hospital or a prison, drugs, diet, counsellors, psychotherapists, spiritual advisors or indeed any number of contacts, studies, or pursuits until we come upon the edge of the end.

Will there be the intensity of an experience like that of Julian of Norwich, of whom it was said: 'Those who truly see and experience God's love in Jesus are those who become more sensitive to human hurt and can respond, mediating God's own compassion'[7]? Or will it, rather, take us many years and many kinds of searchings to discover the depth of our own poverty and the graciousness of the God who deigns to visit us, even through a reading of the *Catechism of the Catholic Church* which said that just as God created everything out of nothing so He can make a new beginning for the sinner (CCC, 298). In other words, just as the people of Israel discovered God to be the Creator of heaven and earth (Gn 1: 1)[8], discovering too that this meant He could help in whatever situation of life a person or a people found themselves, so a glimmer of a sense of God the Creator could be all the "faith" that God asks if He is to act – or it is possible that because of the prayers of others that He takes pity on us. But, as Cardinal Ratzinger said in his little book on the neglected catechesis

---

[7] Ibid., p. 229.

[8] Cf. Francis Etheredge, *Scripture: A Unique Word*: https://www.cambridgescholars.com/product/978-1-4438-6044-4.

on creation[9], we live in a world in which the value of grasping *God as Creator* is eclipsed and needs to be rediscovered and, as such, may be it will be a life-saving rediscovery!

The Way of the Word of God: Starting Points

In the end, then, is there a pain in discovering our poverty that is worth the recognition of it?

'We need strength in dark times – not from ourselves or of other generations but from God. The pattern of life is in constant flux and every moment comes a new and shocking revelation. The only wisdom is "humility" [derived from the Latin word 'humus' meaning ground]. Practising humility in this context of powerlessness opens a person to the liberating possibilities of grace'[10].

---

[9] *In the Beginning*: https://d2y1pz2y630308.cloudfront.net/20434/documents/2019/9/Ratzinger%20In%20the%20Beginning.pdf.

[10] O'Brien, *The Darkness Shall Be the Light*, pp. 155-56.

If a variety of starting points have one point in common, it is humility. To start to grasp that the very struggle we are in to understand ourselves is a struggle like that of being on quicksand: that the more we twist and turn and thrash about the more we find ourselves sinking and the more inevitable it is, as it were, that our sinking simultaneously sinks our hope of surviving. There is a point of beginning, in other words, which, while it may well vary in the concreate circumstances of lived lives, is a point of realization: that I am approaching the lowest point that I can reach and that this is as irreversible as falling: having been defeated in all my attempts at self-analysis, counselling, psychiatric interventions or whatever form of human help had been asked for – even that of vocational searches with those who help us to decide whether or not we have a vocation to the priesthood or to the religious life. In other words, our life experience has shown us that we are in some way unreachable, untouchable by human help, out of touch with our reality to the degree that whatever life-line there seemed to be, whether from an inspiring story, a friendship, yet another course of study or action, these threads seem to disintegrate like so many lines, in a way, which line the direction down and point to a pit.

What word, then, has the power to change going down into going up? Even recently there was a word in the Gospel about Bartimaeus calling out to the Lord, while His disciples wanted him to stop shouting - but Bartimaeus kept shouting out (cf. Mk 10: 46-52). However, let us go to the opening of this moment, as it were, when the Lord starts out. Jesus has just answered His disciples' argument about who is the greatest by calling them to a life of service: 'For the Son of man came not to be served but to serve, and to give his life as a ransom for many' (Mk 10: 45). Following this outcome, St. Mark tells us: 'And they came to Jericho; and as he was leaving Jericho ...' (Mk 10: 46). But Jericho is full of significance! Jericho, where the first battle took place for the promised land[11], which can translate into a starting point for "entering" the new promised land of true discipleship – especially in view of Christ calling Zacchaeus down from the tree. Thus, proceeding from the following dialogue with Zacchaeus: that He 'must stay at your house today' (Lk 19: 5) we discover that Christ is the 'guest of a man who is a sinner' (Lk 19: 7), who changes and, therefore, Christ says, 'salvation has

---

[11] Andrew, "Jericho? Why Jericho?": https://www.pilgrim.org.au/blog/?p=357.

come to this house' (Lk 19: 9). In other words, the disciples had come to the lowest point: the lowest inhabited place on earth[12]: the point of departure from which the vocation to be of service starts with being of service to the sinner – just as Jericho is the lowest point on earth, so this is the lowest point from where service and salvation starts from.

How, then, do we translate our experience of meeting Christ at the lowest point in our lives into helping others?

---

[12] Stephan A, "Jericho – the lowest-situated city in the world": https://www.thiscityknows.com/jericho-the-lowest-situated-city-in-the-world/.

CHAPTER FOUR

ANOREXIA AND THE PULL OF PURPOSE

In this fourth piece, what comes into focus is not only the "sufferer" but those who "suffer with".

From the Greek, *anorexia* means a "loss of appetite" and *nervosa* indicates a non-organic disorder[1]; but, as we shall see, "loss of appetite" is not so simple. Its first diagnosis under the heading *anorexia nervosa*, it seems, was in 1873 and started to multiply, as it were, in the 1950s[2]; in general, we probably think of anorexia as a teenage girl-woman syndrome but apparently a third of sufferers can be male[3]. If this is an accurate account of anorexia's proliferation, then the rise in its incidence gives rise to multiple questions about significant factors. However, in view

---

[1] Cf. "Anorexia Nervosa": https://en.wikipedia.org/wiki/Anorexia_nervosa.

[2] Ibid.

[3] Ibid.

of an excellent autobiographical study by Evanna Lynch[4], this piece will focus on the girl-woman dimension of the condition.

But is it a "leap" too far to go from anorexia, a compulsive[5] condition whereby a woman loses weight to the point of being on the brink of losing her life[6], to so called medical help to kill herself? But then, suddenly, a committee which specialises in helping people to kill themselves has considered a request from a woman suffering from anorexia nervosa who wants help to kill herself[7]. Instead, then, of a committee reviewing all the possible options concerning her life and the implicit, now explicit desire to

---

[4] See the epic autobiographical study called, *The Opposite of Butterfly Hunting: The Tragedy and The Glory of Growing Up: A Memoir*, by Evanna Lynch, London: Headline Publishing Group, 2021.

[5] Ibid., p.255.

[6] Ibid., p. 252.

[7] "Aid in Dying Ethics Consultation Service: Summary of Consultation concerning a Patient with Anorexia Nervosa September 3, 2021": https://www.acamaid.org/wp-content/uploads/2021/09/Ethics-Consultation-Anorexia-Nervosa-9-3-21.pdf.

die, there is a committee reviewing the possibility of help-ing this woman to die.

While some people do die from anorexia[8] and others do go on to plot their way through a maze of what's over the horizon of their illness[9], it seems as if it is a step too far in bringing it into the orbit of loneliness and euthanasia and, by implication, suicide; but, as we have seen, the wid-ening path of permissible killing broadens to the point of opening up what would have been considered a challenge to the imagination to investigate the path through suffer-ing to life. Evanna Lynch says: 'an eating disorder is a mental condition, and so it will never work ... trying to stuff that body with food and squash the eating disorder out'[10]. On the one hand, in view of the mystery of the whole person, the psychosomatic whole of being one in body and soul (*Gaudium et Spes*, 14), an eating disorder goes beyond being simply a problem with eating. In other words, while there are clearly health emergencies from an extreme condition of weight loss, the point remains that

---

[8] Lynch, *The Opposite of Butterfly Hunting*, p. 123.

[9] Ibid., p. 113, 270, 318.

[10] Ibid., p. 68.

the question of the purpose of life is a decisive factor in both the nature of illness and the possibility of recovery.

Social Context: Healing and modern weight loss

The first doctors to diagnose anorexia worked at a time when psychiatric disorders were beginning to be recognized; and, as it happens, a part of the social context is the remarkable fact that a number of the pioneers of psychiatric medicine were both Jewish and doctors and, by implication, were sensitive to the possibility of suffering being significant in a person's life[11]: both because of the

---

[11] Cf. Francis Etheredge, A trilogy: *From Truth to truth: Volume II-Faith and Reason in Dialogue*, Newcastle upon Tyne: Cambridge Scholars Publishing, 2016, p. 137: It has already been noted in passing that a number of modern pioneers of psychoanalysis and psychology were actually Jewish doctors. Josef Breuer (1842-1925) was a doctor, whose father taught in a Jewish community. Sigmund Freud (1856-1939), who is more widely known, was a doctor. Alfred Adler (1870-1937) was a doctor. Erich Fromm (1900-1980), it seems, explicitly linked his study of the Torah with psychological insight[11]. Bruno Bettelheim (1903-1990) was Jewish, devoting himself to the care of children with autism. Abraham Maslow (1908-1970) had

whole history of salvation but also because of specific lives in which God has acted[12]. Perhaps, then, these pioneers were disposed to see that illness had a significance for a person's life and that disposed them to think in terms of a person's symptoms expressing a significance beyond what was apparently presented; however, having said that, the absence of physical causes is also a steppingstone, too, to alternative diagnoses. At the same time as there has been a recognition of the psychosomatic interrelationship of body and soul there has been a growing disassociation between mental and physical illness; and, therefore, there is a tendency for some syllabi to leap frog from Aristotle, in the 4th century before Christ, to Descartes as if a change in methodology meant that all that went before, or in between, was necessarily invalid and unrelated to the

---

Jewish parents; and, by implication, a Jewish background. Silvano Arieti (1914-1981), another doctor, who also wrote explicitly on Abraham.

[12] E.g. Abraham and Sarah, Hannah, Naaman, King Hezekiah, a woman who helped Elijah and Elijah helped etc. etc. Cf. also the healing of a man warned by Christ that something worse would befall him if he sinned again (cf. Jn 5: 1-18, verse 14).

present[13]: as if the existence of the soul is not an ancient realization with modern implications. So, in other words, there is a tendency for all illness to be medicalized as if all illness is wholly physical and organic; and, in the process, the doctor almost becomes a mechanic, employing physical remedies "off the shelf". There needs, then, to be a rediscovery and a reintegration of the whole nature of the human person and "being ill".

When it comes, then, to the two doctors who diagnosed anorexia, there is no mention of an explicit religious faith in the life of one of one of them, Charles Lasègue [14]; however, the other one, Dr. William Gull, did have a Christian background and chose the words

---

[13] Etheredge, *Volume II-Faith and Reason in Dialogue*, 2016, pp. 130-132.

[14] Nerissa Soh, Garry Walter, Michael Robertson, Gin S. Malhi, "Charles Lasègue (1816–1883): beyond anorexie hystérique": https://onlinelibrary.wiley.com/doi/full/10.1111/j.1601-5215.2010.00499.x; and "Sir Withey William Gull, 1st Baronet": https://www.britannica.com/biography/Sir-William-Withey-Gull-1st-Baronet. It is beyond the scope of this essay to discuss whether or not he was Jack the Ripper. By contrast, he supported the education of a woman doctor ("William Gull": https://en.wikipedia.org/wiki/William_Gull).

"Without God, Labour is in Vain" to go on his coat of arms and had a favorite biblical verse on his grave[15]. Both of these doctors, it seems, arrived at their diagnoses empirically and, while treatment was often positive, taking account of family background[16] and the need for dietary supplements, there were fatalities[17]. It was recognized from very early on that the loss of weight led to a cessation, interruption or even the permanent loss of menstruation[18]. Historically, however, there do seem to have been some early diagnoses of excessive weight loss[19].

In the course of these very changing times there is the whole development of modern feminism, not least of which was the work of Edith Stein[20] as well as the more

---

[15] "William Gull".

[16] Cf. "Charles Lasègue": https://en.wikipedia.org/wiki/Charles_Las%C3%A8gue.

[17] "William Gull".

[18] Cf. "William Gull"; and also Lynch, *The Opposite of Butterfly Hunting,* 2021.

[19] "History of anorexia nervosa": https://en.wikipedia.org/wiki/History_of_anorexia_nervosa.

[20] E.g. *Edith Stein: Life in a Jewish Family, 1891-1916,* translated by Josephine Koeppel, OCD, Washington, DC: ICS Publications, 1986.

well known, English and American protagonists of woman's rights. In addition, two world wars and their social upheavals. Then there is the definitely, more modern part of the social context in which anorexia has grown, namely, the fashion turn to thinness with one of the earliest supermodels, "Twiggy", whose slender shape was regarded as an icon in and of the 60s[21]. Later, a prominent and famous female singer, Karen Carpenter, died of complications from an eating disorder and what she was doing to sustain it[22]. All of which prompts the question of whether or not an increase in anorexia was in proportion to the development of teenage magazines, media[23] and especially more recently the social media[24]. On the one

---

[21] Cf. Jeanette L. Nolan, "Twiggy : British Fashion Model": https://www.britannica.com/biography/Twiggy-British-fashion-model; cf. Crystal Karges, "Modeling and Anorexia: Where Have We Been? Where Are We Now?": https://www.eatingdisorderhope.com/information/anorexia/modeling-and-anorexia-where-have-we-been-where-are-we-now.

[22] https://en.wikipedia.org/wiki/Karen_Carpenter.

[23] Cf. Lynch, *The Opposite of Butterfly Hunting,* pp. 33, 39.

[24] Cf. Sarah Marsh, "Women losing their periods because of restrictive diets and excessive exercise": https://www.theguardian.com/society/2022/jan/06/women-

hand, however, there is the background "presence", as it were, of famine afflicted countries and people[25]; but, on the other hand, the incidence of anorexia nervosa seems to be predominantly in affluent countries: 'anorexia nervosa is far more prevalent in the United States, Europe, and industrialized Asia than it is elsewhere in the world'[26].

In a disturbing new trend, moreover, there seems to be an increase among some teenage girls or young women of a less than replacement diet, an intensive routine of physical training and a growing disappearance of periods without, at the same time, a medical recognition that significant weight loss can be the cause of the woman's body being unable to begin or to maintain a menstrual cycle[27]. The significance of the presence of ovulation is that it is a significant indicator of a woman's general health[28]. As we

---

losing-their-periods-because-of-restrictive-diets-and-excessive-exercise

[25] Cf. Lynch, *The Opposite of Butterfly Hunting*, p. 52.

[26] "Anorexia Nervosa: Historical Developments": https://www.britannica.com/science/anorexia-nervosa.

[27] Cf. Sarah Marsh, "Women losing their periods because of restrictive diets and excessive exercise".

[28] Cf. Marguerite R. Duane and Erin Adams, "The State of Fertility Awareness Based Method Education for Medical

come round, as it were, to Evanna Lynch's autobiographical study, we see, too, that Evanna's mother suffered from
anorexia in her teenage years[29]. What is more, it still
seemed as if there was an element of this background present as her mother still tried to 'keep up with all those
Glamazons outside the church'[30]. Evanna, then, who begins her account of anorexia some twenty years ago, was
showing well established symptoms of the relationship between losing weight, exercise and period loss[31].

However, as the Catholic Church is a part of the context of Evanna Lynch's account of her anorexia[32], it is necessary to mention that the Church is undergoing a renewal which has, as a watershed, the *Second Vatican
Council*, between 1962 and 1965, with particular documents like Pope St. Paul VI letter on the transmission of
human life, *Humanae Vitae*, in 1968, and the whole

Professionals", in *Humanae Vitae, 50 Years Later,* edited by
Theresa Notare, 2019, p. 206: ovulation is monitored 'since the
presence of ovulation is a sign of good health' (and see footnote
40: Pilar Vigil et al, *The Linacre Quarterly*, no. 4 2012).

[29] Lynch, *The Opposite of Butterfly Hunting*, p. 133.

[30] Ibid., p. 24.

[31] Ibid., pp. 59, 123.

[32] Ibid., p. 33.

articulation of the truth of this teaching in a more and more contradictory environment of recreational sex, pornography, contraception, abortion and the breakdown of family life. At the same time as the renewal of the Catholic Church is taking place there is a new and violent explosion of anger as reports of the abuse of minors has emerged from different places; and, therefore, there is no doubt that the discrediting of priestly service has had a bearing on people's willingness to draw on the gifts of Christianity. Nevertheless reform, if it is not cosmetic, is about witness to the love of God for the sinner and the fruits of this in our lives.

Circles within circles: Spiraling down or spiraling out?

Clearly, there is some possibility that while society is changing and becoming more self-preoccupied, in the sense of focusing on an outward, bodily shape, rather than the whole person, there is a sense that the internalization of this preoccupation with body size has a kind of language about it which, if it only can be read, would open up the interiority of this problem.

Within, then, society as a whole and its tendencies and changes, there is also the dynamic of family life[33]. Evanna Lynch, and her family, have been very open about the disruption that her anorexia brought about[34], both in terms of the emotional upheavals, the search for a solution, the travelling, the conflicts and the whole challenge of understanding a radical and almost total stripping of her characteristics to the bone, literally, losing her creativity[35], friends and almost her life. But, to persevere with this circle within the circling changes in society Evanna says, her father having realized he did not want to become a priest but a dad whereupon, after a period of travelling, he

> 'became a teacher, met Mum and started a family, but the guilt of leaving seminary followed him, and for many years after, we all paid for his transgressions

---

[33] Cf. "Anorexia Nervosa".

[34] Lynch, *The Opposite of Butterfly Hunting,* p. 460: a debt of gratitude to her parents, sisters, and brother, for allowing accounts of their family life in the course of addressing Evanna's anorexia (and others too).

[35] Ibid., p. 66.

against God by sacrificing our Sunday mornings to the mind-numbing ritual of Mass'[36].

On the one hand, as a Catholic infant who, while brought up a Catholic, converted to Catholicism at 40, who then married and founded a family, I understand very well the ongoing challenge of our children in the course of transmitting the dynamic nature of the Christian faith to them[37]. But, on the other hand, the impression one receives in Evanna's book is that of a somewhat unarticulated faith which, as it were, goes on being a quiet but impressive presence in the lives of the parents but which does not appear to have been explored in a way that engages the children with the word of God, the Liturgy, and the community of the Church[38].

Furthermore, there does seem to be a very "emotionally charged" exchange in view of dad's problem of being

---

[36] Ibid., p. 33.

[37] See, *The Family on Pilgrimage, The Prayerful Kiss, Honest Rust and Gold, Within Reach of You* etc. etc. all published by En Route Books and Media.

[38] Cf. for example, the New Movements, particularly that of the Neocatechumenal Way.

unable to grow enough potatoes to feed the family[39] which, as I know from experience, is very difficult because of the worms which hollow out what grows to the point of almost harvesting eggshells! One wonders, along with the tendency of the dad to withdraw from helping to discuss sensitive issues, like rape[40], if there is a certain sense in which the dad's priestly formation seems to have been a very "underused" religious resource in their family life. Notwithstanding the difficulties of discussing these sensitive subjects, there is still a lot that can be done to help people understand the reality of sin and salvation; nevertheless, in the absence of her father's response, Evanna's mother invariably manages a helpful response to these difficult questions.

Womanhood? A narrow vision?

There is a sense of the philosophy, now more prevalent, that anyone can become anything, when Evanna says: 'I'm going to be a blue butterfly with patterns, or a

---

[39] Lynch, *The Opposite of Butterfly Hunting*, p. 47-49.
[40] Ibid., pp. 1-10.

pink stripy cat or a white pony with purple hair'[41]. But, following her mother saying that a girl becoming a woman is 'just science'[42], Evanna thought that 'science' entailed 'brutal, uncompromising restraints on ... [her] imagination'[43]. After all, she was 'designing alternate worlds ... [that she could] step into'. Whereas others could 'all grow into buxom women and make their desperate bids for power and husbands'[44] in 'sleepy, rural Ireland'[45].

Evanna does seem to have a particularly negative focus on woman, raising the question of whether her view of "womanhood" has had a bearing on the development of her *anorexia nervosa*. On the one hand she writes very positively about women[46], and about her mother throughout the book[47]; but, on the other hand, there is a distinct sense of womanhood being like growing into a dead end: 'Cliodhna and Mum .... had ended up as mere ladies on couches .... rather than dancing – childless, jobless,

---

[41] Ibid., p. 15.

[42] Ibid., p. 16.

[43] Ibid., p. 16.

[44] Ibid., pp. 29, and 30, 32.

[45] Ibid., p. 91.

[46] Ibid., pp. 17-18.

[47] Ibid., pp. 1-2, 22.

carefree …. not [thinking] creatively enough about their potential and now they were trapped in their lady-bodies'[48]. Moreover, Evanna goes on to say: 'out of the 8.7 million forms of life on earth, I'd been born into the most mundane of them all'[49]. Although there is a spark of the possibility that she wants to be an actress[50], and being an actress would allow her to be a 'mermaid' a 'Jigglypuff' and various other things she also said, very emphatically, 'I didn't want to be any kind of woman'[51].

It is as if there is something about the possibility of being a woman which is equivalent to the closing down of possibilities, not just that it would be difficult to be something desirable but that it would be impossible to be something that Evanna wanted to be. This makes her anorexia a kind of subliminal attempt to eradicate her femininity in a radical way; and, while not particularly conscious, it suggests a real and growing repudiation of women: 'I didn't

---

[48] Ibid., p. 15.

[49] Ibid., p. 16.

[50] Ibid., p. 24.

[51] Ibid., p. 17.

hate them yet'[52] – but that seemed to be where this disorder was leading.

At the same time, however, as the identity of being a woman seemed to be the problem, defining growing up as a kind of suffocating simplicity, it was Evanna's mother who tirelessly fought for a way to help her daughter out of her straight-jacketing illness[53] which, left to itself, was tending beyond the frustration of her natural development, the stripping of her body weight, creativity[54] and friendships, to the possibility of her death.

More personally: The interiority

So, perhaps, anorexia is a new development in terms of a relationship between a background sense of guilt and food. Although there is some suggestions of earlier diagnoses, prior to the 19th century, there seems to be an exponential increase in eating disorders and, particularly, in anorexia. But, in a historical investigation, the difference between religious fasting and anorexia is not to be

---

[52] Ibid., p. 17.

[53] Ibid., pp. 53-62, 62, 69, 72, 93-113, 115-117, 125.

[54] Ibid., p. 68.

overlooked[55]; and, therefore, even now, there can be genuine, religious fasting, which is not about "thinness" but about the triple appeal to God of prayer, fasting and almsgiving. But, nevertheless, maybe there are other, more subtle factors at work, as Evanna says, implicitly: 'I didn't feel I deserved cake or love anymore, and felt a thrum of satisfaction, a faint and interesting pleasure in rejecting them'[56]; and later, after eating a sandwich one day, she says afterwards that it was a 'day of sinfulness'[57]. At the same time as these references to a kind of displaced emphasis on the sin of eating what is not even an ordinary meal but is, in fact, food necessary for her life, there are numerous and intermittent references to a sense of her 'worthlessness'[58].

On the one hand there is an acknowledgment of food as expressing love – but involving the problem of "deserving love": as if love cannot be "undeserved" – just as the gift of human life is totally gratuitous; and, on the other hand, there is the significance of there being 'a thrum of

---

[55] Cf. "Anorexia Nervosa".

[56] Lynch, *The Opposite of Butterfly Hunting*, p. 42.

[57] Ibid., p. 115.

[58] Ibid., pp. 40, 42, 64 83, 271-272, 282, 288.

satisfaction, a faint and interesting pleasure in rejecting [the cakes]'. In other words, what is the 'thrum of satisfaction' about if not some kind of hidden "power" which, ironically, Evanna seemed to regard as a preoccupation of the womanhood she rejects: the preoccupation with 'bids for power and husbands'[59].

What is the nature of this personal power? Is it pride? Because the whole emphasis is on the enclosure of the "self" in a preoccupation with food and 'the prominence of our own hip bones'[60]: as if the refusal of food symbolizes a life-refusal of help, suggesting a self-sufficiency that is as unrealistic as it is, literally, deadly. Even when Evanna is hospitalized and eats a little, she scarcely understands either the seriousness of her illness or the extent of her parent's love, saying, almost unintelligibly, 'They can go back to feeling like good parents again, and I can carry on with my life'[61]. Thus there is not only a kind of disconnectedness between herself and the reality of her declining health to the point that she is now in danger of dying, but there is also a disconnectedness concerning her parent's love: as

---

[59] Ibid., p. 29.

[60] Ibid., p. 283.

[61] Ibid., p. 119.

if it is just about them 'feeling like good parents'. Albeit, later, there is both a temptation to self-harm as a form of punishing her parents – but there is also the emerging desire of the dream of 'acting and performing'[62].

The dream of acting and the whole process by which it comes about is very striking and involves the dedicated support of Evanna's father[63] and mother. There is also the willingness of the acting company to go forward with her, particularly when her problem of anorexia has come to light[64] which, however, does not obstruct her clear grasp of the character that she auditions for and succeeds in playing. Clearly, and Evanna is emphatic in stressing this, the progress from illness to health is not linear, nevertheless there is a definite pull in the direction of acting which, as it is realized, is a real motivation into life beyond the difficulties of an eating disorder.

Naturalism and its unresolved questions

---

[62] Ibid., pp. 270-279, 281.

[63] Ibid., pp. 333-342 etc.

[64] Ibid., pp. 362-363 etc.

It is, then, very courageous of Evanna Lynch to advance this autobiographical study to help fellow sufferers from anorexia[65]; and, at the same time, it is necessary to reflect on the overall impression that arises out of it. Evanna's account takes two directions: her naturalism and her parents Catholicism. There is her own, almost naturalistic account of the pull of purpose: the overarching goal of acting becoming a reality, entailing a reasonable diet and the health and concentration that comes with it; and, in view of her absorption in the part and her general knowledge of the books and particular role, all come together, with those with whom she works, at all levels, to bring about a decisive development in her life in becoming the actress she wanted to be. But, at the same time, there are the enduring questions about life's purpose: 'Why are we even here?' and 'What is it all for?'[66]. And perhaps these are the more permanent questions of purpose which take us beyond illness and what motivates us to what, more deeply, our life about? Thus, in a sense, to have come this far is really only to make a new beginning; and, perhaps, to explore that Catholic Faith which

---

[65] Ibid., pp. ix-xiii.

[66] Ibid., 319, but here 423.

sustained Evanna's parents through their long vigil in the course of their daughter's illness.

This is the other direction of the book: her parents' Catholicism. As we know from the brief mentions so far, irrespective of Evanna's reaction to it[67], the Catholic Faith has been an ongoing and sustaining, steadying and somewhat inspirational influence on her parents' accompanying Evanna throughout her illness, right from her mother's grasp of its incipient beginnings with a "healthy" diet and the rise of an exercise regimen. There is, too, both the prayerful and the practical help that they received from the 'Sisters of Charity'[68]; and, indeed, as Evanna recognizes, while others 'are all giving up on me' her parents 'don't give up' on her[69].

While, then, the faith-life of her parents is largely unexpressed and implicit throughout the whole book, including the involvement and prayerfulness of others, notably the religious sisters, it is nevertheless clear that

---

[67] Ibid., p. 174: Following hospitalization again, Evanna writes: 'There are no more Mass Cards …. I have essentially nullified everyone's efforts over the summer'.

[68] Ibid., pp. 251, but here 294.

[69] Ibid., pp. 175, 311.

without their persevering help there may well have been a very different outcome to Evanna's life struggle. In its own way the perseverance of her parents provides a sign of the fruit of their faith; and, as such, a faith which still remains to be fruitful in Evanna's own life. For, throughout the whole timespan of the book, which is some twenty years, there is a simple presence of her parents and the ongoing nature of her family life; and, as simple as it seems, the faith-life of her parents can be described as an implicit participation in the mystery of the cross of Jesus Christ. The many disappointments and setbacks of the whole experience of Evanna's illness being transformed, if not transfigured, in an almost resurrection turning-about of their daughter into life from the depths of her illness – but not only that but also her parents' persevering love shining through everything and to the end.

CHAPTER FIVE

DEATH[1] AND THE WHOLENESS
OF HUMAN PERSONHOOD

What comes next if not a definition of death? And, by implication, a definition of death involves a definition of life? Thus we come closer to an account of the whole person and, as such, a watershed: we proceed by way of gathering some of what we have already considered and, at the same time, we are re-expressing the context of our discussion to be what suffering reveals and requires of the whole human being and his or her community.

A variety of points – the same conclusion

First: The universal, ancient and primary principle of practical action is 'that good is to be done and pursued

---

[1] Another, entirely different version of this essay, appeared as Chapter Ten: Part IV: "Can the Living Be Dead? The Question Needs an Authoritative Answer!", pp. 99-101, of *Volume III: Faith Is Married Reason*, Newcastle upon Tyne: Cambridge Scholars Publishing, 2016.

and evil avoided' …. so the law in us by nature commands whatever conserves human life and opposes death'[2]. Contrary to many voluntary declarations[3] there is a growing contravention of the principle: do good; avoid harm. If there is any credibility to a medical act then it is because it intends a good. What is the so called good of euthanasia? To supposedly end a person's suffering. But, as we have seen, the deliberate killing of a human being does not end suffering but causes the suffering entailed in killing a person whose heart may in fact be sound and prove difficult to stop. At the same time, there is a complete absence of accompanying the real needs of the person: to be accompanied in seeking to understand the meaning of suffering. Therefore, there is a deliberate contravention of the command to conserve 'human life'. What this reveals, then, is that the desire for death, and indeed definitions of it, can

---

[2] St. Thomas Aquinas, *Summa Theologiae*, translated and edited by Timothy McDermott, OP, London: Methuen, 1989, reprinted 1992; p. 287: Pt. I-II, Qu 94, art. 2.

[3] Cf. Roberto Andorno, Chapter 5: "The Right to Science and the Evolution of Scientific Integrity" of *The Right to Science: Then and Now*: https://www.cambridge.org/core/books/right-to-science/right-to-science-and-the-evolution-of-scientific-integrity/690D1992F0C0756FC2758FFCE5540262.

be self-serving; that is, they can serve purposes other than that of the good of the person who is suffering. In other words, bringing about a person's death can constitute a financial saving, a type of research on how to kill, or a definition of death, like brain death, that can be used to provide organs to recipients for financial gain – all of which conforms to the person's desire to die and none of which contradicts it with a call to life!

In general, then, 'Scientific research, even if motivated by the best of intentions, cannot be conducted in ways that involve the violation of people's dignity (for instance, medical research cannot be conducted without participants' free and informed consent)'[4], thus excluding any kind of coercive or deceptive practice.

What about, then, a subject consenting to a scheme involving their direct killing because it "plays into" the person's sense of being a "waste of space", "worthless", or "unwanted" – all of which may be a direct consequence of how those around the person are responding to them i.e. negatively, giving the person no reason for hope or the

---

[4] Andorno, Chapter 5: "The Right to Science and the Evolution of Scientific Integrity" of *The Right to Science: Then and Now*.

encouragement to live. In other words, those around the person seeking to die are directly contributing to the desire to die and, in due course, bringing it about; for example:

> 'She [the man's wife] found out that the one nurse in palliative care had spoken to him for two hours in the middle of the night, convincing him that ... [being killed] was the right thing to do"[5].

Clearly, then, there is an implicit coercion on the part of those who agree with and advance, the deliberate killing of people with the underlying "emotional" complexion of those who want to die.

To deliberately stop the heart

In the course of discussing euthanasia, the deliberate act of bringing about a person's death, there arose the admission from a doctor who specialized in studying this

---

[5] Alex Schadenberg "Is Death Becoming an Industry in Canada?": https://alexschadenberg.blogspot.com/2021/11/is-death-becoming-industry-in-canada.html.

event that it was necessary to stop the heart in order to bring about death:

> '"We're learning. Hypothesis, data and confirmation. This is what science is," he said. "Our job is to stop the heart; that's what they want us to do"'[6].

Second: Since when did "science" exist without the scientist's conscience determining whether or not what he is doing is right or wrong; and, in the absence of a scientist acting uprightly, where is the judgement of others about his conduct? Are not these the discrepancies that led to the Nuremburg trials of Nazi war criminals[7], the

---

[6] "Doctors seek life-ending drugs that smooth the way for the terminally ill" by Lisa M. Krieger: https://medicalx-press.com/news/2020-09-doctors-life-ending-drugs-smooth-terminally.html.

[7] P. 11, footnote 19, from Dr. Mary Anne Urlakis' "General Foreword" to Francis Etheredge's *The Human Person: A Bio-ethical Word*, St. Louis, MO: En Route Books and Media, 2017: 'Vivien Spitz, was the youngest court reporter at the Nuremberg Trials, and personally recorded more than 300,000 pages of testimony during the War Crimes Trials. Her memoir, *Doctors from Hell*, documents these atrocities. Sentient Publishing,

mistreatment of syphilis patients in America[8] and the abuse of Puerto Rican women in the trialing of hormonal contraceptive compounds[9]? In other words, even though there are several ethical declarations, endorsing the specific ways that people need protection from conception onwards, there are multiple ways that the so called scientific and business community has transgressed, and continues to transgress, the rights of human beings to life, conceived through the reciprocal self-gift of husband and wife, to therapeutic interventions for their own good, to completing human development, and to the welfare of the

---

2005, Boulder, Colorado. Cf. also Roberto Andorno, Chapter 5, I, of *The Right to Science: Then and Now*: this and the following two were inhumanely coercive and did not involve the proper consent of the subjects.

[8] Urlakis, "General Foreword", Etheredge's *The Human Person: A Bioethical Word*, pp. 13-16.

[9] Cf. "*Humanae Vitae*: My testimony as a doctor" by Philippe Schepens, General Secretary of the World Federation of Doctors who Respect Human Life, delivered at "*Humanae Vitae* at 50: Setting the Context", Pontifical University of St Thomas Aquinas, Rome, 28 Oct 2017: http://voiceofthefamily.com/dr-phillippe-schepens-humanae-vitae-a-medical-doctors-testimony/.

whole human person expressing the "priority of the person" in all that concerns their integral spiritual, psychological and physical good. In other words, the good of the human person is a triple good; and, without a consideration of all three dimensions, they are being reductively reduced to whatever "force" has coercive control of them.

Science, then, is no more ethically free than a human being who is a scientist is ethically free; but, on the other hand, the candid admission that the stopping of the heart is necessary for a declaration of death raises the possibility that "brain death" is not death. In other words, being able to claim that brain death is death has a definite implication that it is for the sake of organ transplantation – which will certainly bring about death – rather than for the benefit of determining whether or not the potential donor is dead. Is "brain death", then, covert euthanasia? Clearly, if it was not for the massive use of drugs to bring about death, the body of the dead person could have been used for organ transplantation; and, therefore, one can almost speak of death by deliberate killing as a contamination of the possible good arising out of a person's natural death.

Third: Both in general and because of the uncertainty about how a particular person will react to the drugs which are given to end a person's life, there is an element of the experimental in the action of deliberating killing him or her; and, because of this, there cannot be a convincing claim that the death will be clinically controlled – rather there is always a risk of an indefinite delay in the process of death itself. But, in addition, from the blatant claim of those who are trying to kill a person, there is the admission that unless they 'stop the heart' then there is no death. In other words, it is quite clear to the people who are killing a person that death is not established except by stopping the heart, irreversibly. In other words, there is no attempt to bring about 'brain death', nor is 'brain death' deemed death; rather, the beating heart is taken to be the key organ that determines the life of the whole person and, therefore, stopping the heart is the explicit objective.

Death and life: their interrelationship: two quotations

The following, contrasting positions, as expressed by a modern Catholic philosopher, express the challenge in our time of addressing the differentiation, if there is to be any, between death and brain death. The following two quotes help to set the scene for this part of the discussion; the first quotation:

'... [T]he chairman of the German Bishops' Conference years ago in connection with the debate about so-called brain death explained that while it could be that brain death is not the death of the human being, in any case it would be the death of the person'[10].

A test is limited to what it can do: it reveals and conceals

Fourth: The Bishop said, *'while it could be that brain death is not the death of the human being, in any case it would be the death of the person.'* Thus the question is posed: is there a real distinction between the life of the person and the death of the brain? In other words, is the person dead if there is a living human being who is 'brain dead'? If, then, the so called death of the brain does not bring about the stopping of the heart then, according to the doctors who kill people, the person is not dead. The

---

[10] Spaemann Robert. 2012. b. "Was macht Personen zu Personen?" *Philosophisches Jahrbuch* 119: 10-11; cited as a part of the following paper: Elinor Gardner, "Unpacking Robert Spaemann's Philosophical Contribution to the Brain Death Debate": Linacre Q. 2019 Nov; 86(4): 381–393: Published online: https://www.ncbi.nlm.nih.gov/pmc/articles/PMC6880064/ .

distinction, posed by the Bishop, between a living 'human being' who is, at the same time, expressing the 'death of the person' because of being brain dead, is a distinction which has been introduced into the "wholeness" of human personhood; and, therefore, the possibility of the distinction between a living human being, who is dead, being real, depends on the possibility of the fragmentation of the wholeness of human being. What, philosophically, justifies the fragmentation of the wholeness of human being – Is it simply that the claim that this is possible is its justification? In other words, what is the evidence, or metaphysical justification, for declaring a living human being alive but expressing the death of the person? The significant criterion is so called 'brain death'.

On the one hand, it is clear that a person lives in so far as there are vital signs of life, including autonomous heart and lung activity; and, therefore, in the absence of these it is not necessary to maintain them artificially, in that extraordinary or burdensome treatments are not ethically and pastorally necessary. Therefore, assuming autonomous functions, even if the brain is so called "electrically dead", entails the realization that the person is alive. The threshold for electrical activity is called 'a flat EEG called [an] isoelectric line, ... [and] is presumed to be associated with silenced activity in cortical neurons'[11]. At the same time, however, we know that resuscitation is possible even if the heart has stopped beating. This is mentioned, however, not because of heart activity being a standalone indicator of human life, but just by way of recognition that death is not automatically a "moment". As regards brain activity, the key measurement of brain electrical activity is undertaken by an electroencephalogram[12]; and, as explained in the following excerpt, is a part of the 'brain death' definition:

'The electroencephalogram (EEG) reflects brain electrical activity. A flat (isoelectric) EEG, which is usually recorded during very deep coma, is considered to be a turning point between a living brain and a deceased brain. Therefore the isoelectric EEG constitutes, together with evidence of irreversible structural brain

---

[11] Kroeger D, Florea B, Amzica F (2013) "Human Brain Activity Patterns beyond the Isoelectric Line of Extreme Deep Coma". PLoS ONE 8(9): e75257. https://doi.org/10.1371/journal.pone.0075257.

[12] Cf. "isoelectric electroencephalogram": https://medical-dictionary.thefreedictionary.com/isoelectric+electroencephalogram.

damage, one of the criteria for the assessment of brain death'[13].

The authors of the aforementioned report go on to argue the following:

'The results presented ... [in this paper] challenge the common wisdom that the isoelectric line is always associated with absent cerebral activity, and demonstrate[s] that the isoelectric line is not necessarily one of the ultimate signs of a dying brain'[14].

What emerges is the following: that the baseline of electrical activity, the 'isoelectric line' is more a reflection of the limitations of the monitoring method of brain activity – than a definitive reading of *no brain activity*.

A test result is a partial account of a whole

Following the previous discussion of the Bishop's claim, '*while it could be that brain death is not the death of*

---

[13] Kroeger *et al*, "Human Brain Activity Patterns".
[14] Ibid.

the human being, in any case it would be the death of the person', it is now necessary to go on and to discuss the second quotation:

> *'I would like to argue against this conception and to defend the thesis that personhood is not a quality but is the being of a human being and therefore begins no later than the existence of a new human life not identical with the parental organism'[15].*

The principle now under discussion is twofold, as it were: that *'personhood is not a quality but is the being of a human being'* and, therefore, that personhood begins with the beginning *'of a new human life not identical with the parental organism'*.

Fifth: The fact that there can be electrical activity in the brain below the 'isoelectric line' is very significant in

---

[15] Spaemann Robert. 2012. b. "Was macht Personen zu Personen?" *Philosophisches Jahrbuch* 119: 10-11; cited as a part of the following paper: Elinor Gardner, "Unpacking Robert Spaemann's Philosophical Contribution to the Brain Death Debate": Linacre Q. 2019 Nov; 86(4): 381–393: Published online: https://www.ncbi.nlm.nih.gov/pmc/articles/PMC6880064/ .

that it indicates that the brain is still a part of the whole of human personhood; for, if there is autonomous functioning of the heart and lungs, then it follows that the psychosomatic whole is still integrated, even in the absence of evidence for specific functions at the time – for the brain, while an overarching central organ of the nervous system, is nevertheless a biologically dependent organ for nutrition and, as it were, the basic impulse and energy, however minimal, of life itself. In other words, the very evidence of minimal electrical activity is evidence of the integrity of the whole organism: of the integrity of the human being as a whole. Furthermore, in terms of what is possible, precisely because the integrity of the person is intact, it is unclear whether or not further cerebral cortex activity is recoverable:

> 'a rudiment of oscillatory activity might persist in subcortical neurons. Whether this activity can become synchronized and re-emerge at the cortical level is so far unknown'[16].

---

[16] Kroeger *et al*, (2013) "Human Brain Activity Patterns".

Life and death interpret each other

Life, in its spiritual and somatic unity, commands our respect[17]. [Death] 'occurs when the spiritual principle which ensures the unity of the individual can no longer exercise its functions in and upon the organism, whose elements, left to themselves, disintegrate'[18]. 'The moment of ... [death] is not directly discernible, and the problem is to identify its signs'[19].

Sixth: The reality, then, that the integrity of the whole person persists, even if there is minimal brain activity, is an objective psychosomatic fact; and, in that psychological activity is dependent on somatic activity, it follows that while the somatic activity is relatively dormant so will the psychological activity be too. However, subliminal or semi-dormant activity is not death; rather, it is the

---

[17] Pope St. John Paul II, "Address to the Working Group on 'The Determination of Brain Death and its Relationship to Human Death", article 2, Pope St. John Paul II cited *Gaudium et Spes*, 14, 27: https://www.pas.va/en/magisterium/saint-john-paul-ii/1989-14-december.html.

[18] St. John Paul II, "Address to the Working Group" etc., article 4.

[19] Ibid.

psychosomatic whole's default response to impaired functioning and trauma. Just as, from conception, physical and physiological development precedes psychological development, the former the presupposition of the latter, so deterioration of the physical, physiological expression of human being impairs but does not eradicate the possibility of a person's psychological expressibility. Thus it is now necessary to consider the origin of the psychosomatic whole of human personhood.

Seventh: What is the definition of life? Human life is transmitted from the first instant of fertilization, entailing as it does a flow of calcium ions from what was the sperm, and which begins the process of conception, inconclusively culminating in the fusion of the egg and the sperm's nuclei and the ongoing embryonic development which unfolds from then on. The outward sign of the first instant of fertilization, presumably an effect of the calcium ions flooding across what was the egg's surface, is the formation of the embryonic wall from, as it were, the closing of the pores which, prior to this, were the possible "ports" of the sperm; and, in so far as this is virtually instant on the sperm's entering an outer entrance in the outward layer of the ovum, this is the moment of transformation: the first outward expression of the beginning of the whole human being. And just as any other developmental stage is a part of a sequence, so is conception, both completing its own stepped progress from the first instant of fertilization to the fusion of the sperm and egg's nuclei, so development then seamlessly continues through the subsequent stages of human development until, gradually, somatic development facilitates the expression of psychological development. In other words, it is not a fault if movement, which is both physical and psychological, cannot be expressed because the requisite developmental stage has not been reached; it is, rather, an expression of developmental time that one stage advances on a previous one and provides a foundation for what is still to come.

At the same time as there is an integrity to human being there is an implicit interiority which shows forth in the course of human development, manifesting the capacities of the person; however, being a person is itself the primary manifestation of human being and, subsequently, the psychological gifts, personality and character traits are expressed and formed through life experience. What this implies, then, is that just as thought transcends matter but is embodied in communication and artifacts, so the soul, the life of the body, which makes possible the transcendence of matter, is embodied in the body which expresses it; and, just as biological matter cannot give itself what goes beyond itself, so God creates and infuses the human soul at the first instant of fertilization – thus enabling the integral unfolding of the whole person from then onwards.

In conclusion, just as life and death interpret one another, so both of them elude the perception of the precise moment of their occurrence; but, in view of the reality of the first instant of true fertilization and the first instant of actual death, they nevertheless take place: both because the psychosomatic whole of the person has come to exist and, subsequently, because the integrity of that psychosomatic whole of the human person has ceased to exist. Life and death, while essentially different moments of a single human life, nevertheless mirror each other and manifest what is beyond our grasp but within the reach of our understanding. Signs of electrical life, whether the flow of calcium ions at the first instant of fertilization or the abiding presence of electrical activity in the autonomous human being, however unconscious, are signs of integral, human, personal life from beginning to end.

Therefore, from the moral point of view, when we are expressly required to 'conserve [autonomous] human life', it is not a good action to intentionally end his or her life; and, pastorally, the person and their relatives may need help to bear with the difficulties of living the final stages of life before death takes its own natural course. On the one hand, while refraining from drawing a person prematurely into death, it is necessary nevertheless to prepare for death. On the other hand, while welcoming the life remaining, it is not necessary to enact a burdensome treatment in the final steps to death – but to prayerfully help prepare the person to meet his or her Lord.

CHAPTER SIX

BRAIN DEATH AND THE LIFE AND DEATH OF CHRIST[1]: CAN THE LIVING BE DEAD?

Death is a whole and needs elucidating by the death of Christ.

'The new definition of death as "brain death" makes it possible to declare people dead while they are still breathing and to bypass the dying process in order to quarry spare parts for the living from the dying'[2].

'According to the surgeons, [who had transplanted a pig's kidney into the body of a 'brain-death-diagnosed

---

[1] Another version of this essay appeared as Chapter Ten: Part IV: "Can the Living Be Dead? The Question Needs an Authoritative Answer!", pp. 99-101, of *Volume III: Faith Is Married Reason*, Newcastle upon Tyne: Cambridge Scholars Publishing, 2016.

[2] R. Spaemann, "When Death Becomes Inhuman", *Communio: International Catholic Review*, 33 (Summer 2006), p. 299 of pp. 298-300.

person'] everything worked well for three days. However, this fact contradicts everything that could be said in favor of the definition of brain-death, because it would be impossible to a make a donated organ – even, as in this case, when coming from a pig – work in a dead person'[3].

Thus it is evident that just as the definition of the moment of conception[4] requires an intensive examination of

---

[3] Weimann, *Bioethical Challenges* at the *End of Life*, p. 194, citing footnote 101, Nancy Lipid, "U.S. surgeons" etc; but cf. also the extensive work of Doyen Nguyen, *The New Definitions of Death for Organ Donation: A Multidisciplinary Analysis from the Perspective of Christian Ethics*, published by Peter Lang AG, *Internationaler Verlag der Wissenschaften*; New edition (April 18, 2018: https://www.amazon.com/Definitions-Death-Organ-Donation-Multidisciplinary/dp/3034332777.

[4] Cf. Relevant essays in the first collection: *Scripture: A Unique Word*, Cambridge Scholars, 2014; Chapter 5 of *Mary and Bioethics: An Exploration*: https://enroutebooksandmedia.com/maryandbioethics/; and particularly Profs. Justo Aznar and Julio Tudela's contribution to Chapter 5 of *Conception: An Icon of the Beginning*: https://enroutebooksandmedia.com/conception/; and, in addition, Chapter 7 of *The Human Person: A Bioethical Word*: https://enroutebooksandmedia.com/bioethicalword/.

the evidence in the light of philosophical and theological principles, as indeed does the transmission of human life, so does the definition of death require an equally sensitive answer to modern developments and concerns.

The natural law prompts us to do good

Nothing has changed about the command to do 'whatever conserves human life and opposes death', albeit that does not oblige us to use extraordinary measures to preserve human life. At the same time, the Church has increasingly, and now more definitively, expressed her opposition to the death penalty as a punishment in favor of the possibility of the criminal genuinely renouncing his crime and hoping in God: 'Lastly, more effective systems of detention have been developed, which ensure the due protection of citizens but, at the same time, do not definitively deprive the guilty of the possibility of redemption'[5].

---

[5] "New revision of number 2267 of the Catechism of the Catholic Church on the death penalty – Rescriptum "ex Audentia SS.mi", 02.08.2018": https://press.vatican.va/content/ salastampa/en/bollettino/pubblico/2018/08/02/180802a.html; and cf. also: Letter to the Bishops regarding the new revision of number 2267 of the Catechism of the Catholic Church on the

But we also live in a world where the threshold of bringing about the death of a person is no longer, automatically, a transgression against the first principle of human action: do good, avoid evil, whereby 'the law in us by nature commands whatever conserves human life and opposes death'[6]. Indeed, the irony is inescapable that one person is imprisoned for killing another and another person is lauded for doing so. Thus our understanding of death suffers from the possibility of being wrapped in ulterior motives and the technology necessary for harvesting organs, although it can be the case that a person is clearly dead and it is a help to others to receive the organs of the person who has just died.

So the question posed here, presupposing our obligation to 'conserve human life'[7], is what constitutes death

---

death penalty, from the Congregation for the Doctrine of the Faith, 02.08.2018: https://press.vatican.va/content/salas-tampa/en/bollettino/pubblico/2018/08/02/180802b.html.

[6] St. Thomas Aquinas, *Summa Theologiae*, translated and edited by Timothy McDermott, OP, London: Methuen, 1989, reprinted 1992; p. 287: Pt. I-II, Qu 94, art. 2.

[7] There are five articles to be published on the Catholic Medical Quarterly website, UK, beginning with the February edition, which explore "Aloneness, Euthanasia, The Meaning

and, indeed, does the death of Jesus Christ illuminate the nature of death for all of us? Thus this is not an examination of how Christ's death is salvific for us, which it is and entails a very different kind of discussion; rather, this is an exploration of what His death reveals about human death and, therefore, whether it is true to say that brain death is the death of the whole person[8].

Do life and death interpret each other?

Can death speak to us of life? In other words, is "bodily life" the same thing as the "life" of a person? Indeed what kind of life is life? If, from the moment of human conception there is a progressive manifestation of the life of a person, then where there is human life there is the life of a human person.

In conversation with a man of the street who, unfortunately, has subsequently died from his injuries from

of Life, Anorexia and Brain Death"; go to the CMQ website for updates: http://www.cmq.org.uk/Current-Issue-Contents.html

[8] I am indebted to a one-time colleague, Mr, now Deacon Dr. Bernard Farrell-Roberts, for sharing his thoughts on the question of the definition of death and thus, indirectly, prompting me to these reflections.

soldiering in Afghanistan, he concurred and expressed in his own way that "where there is life there is electrical activity". So, for example, where there is a microbe, plant or animal life, there is electrical activity. However, the converse is not necessarily true in that there can be an electrical storm but no actual biological life. So, although it is equally difficult to determine the precise moment of life and death[9], there is nevertheless evidence for both. In the case of the first instant of human fertilization, owing to the contact between the sperm and the egg, there is a flow of calcium ions from sperm to egg and the closing of what is now the embryonic wall, indicating the beginning of an autonomous human person, one in body and soul[10]. In the case of death, because the electrical activity of the brain is dependent on the life of the whole person, where there is bodily life there is the life of the person; and, therefore, death is not definitive until there is, literally, no

---

[9] Cf. Pope St. John Paul II, "Address to the Working Group on 'The Determination of Brain Death and its Relationship to Human Death", article 4, Pope St. John Paul II cited *Gaudium et Spes*, 14, 27: https://www.pas.va/en/magisterium/saint-john-paul-ii/1989-14-december.html.

[10] Cf. *Gaudium et Spes*, 14 for the person's psychosomatic unity.

autonomous human life. In other words, brain death is not death itself, if by brain death there is understood to be electrical activity beyond the threshold of what is normally detectable[11]; and, as such, this is indicative of the reciprocal relationship between the body as the natural environment of the brain and the brain as the "vehicle" of the subjectivity of the person.

If the first instant of life is an "outward" expression of an inward mystery, namely God giving the gift of an ensouled human soul (cf. *Humanae Vitae*, 13), then death is an outward expression of an inward mystery: the sundering of what is intrinsically inseparable. And, just as life is expressed in the activities of human life, so death comes when the activities of human life have ceased. Just as the beginning of life is manifest in the activity of the whole body, so death is necessarily an end to the activity of the whole body. If the dying process is not complete, then the life of the person is present. In other words, death cannot

---

[11] Kroeger D, Florea B, Amzica F (2013) "Human Brain Activity Patterns beyond the Isoelectric Line of Extreme Deep Coma". PLoS ONE 8(9): e75257. https://doi.org/10.1371/journal.pone.0075257. This is explored more fully in article 5 of a series to be run in the Catholic Medical Quarterly, UK, from the February issue, 2022.

come to the bodily person, except that it comes to the bodily person as a whole. Moreover, in view of resuscitation, the manual or electric restarting of the heart, there is clearly a kind of "window" in the moment of death which is, as it were, open to life returning to the body that it has not, as it were, completely left; and, in view of the contrast between death and life, life is clearly the life of the person. In other words, it is not a body that is brought back to life it is, Sheila, Martin or Lazarus (cf. Jn 11: 43-44); and, indeed, this is not a resurrection of the body – but some kind of recovery of mortal, human life, for the chief priests 'planned to put Lazarus ... to death' (Jn 11: 10).

Furthermore, if the bodily life of a human person is a living expression of the interpersonal "gift" of life, then the "lifeless corpse" is an interpersonal sign of the death of the person. Thus the dead body points to the mystery of life and to the continuation of the relationships through which we originated; indeed, the very "incarnation", as it were, of the embodiment of the soul in the flesh of human life[12] manifests the totality of interrelationships of which we are an expression: to the universe, to each other and to

---

[12] Cf. Pope St. John Paul II, *Familiaris Consortio*, 11; and cf. also *Gaudium et Spes*, 14.

God – all of which will be a part of what is transfigured at the end of time[13].

The philosophical interface: between life and death

The theme of relationship steps in philosophically, as it were, between life and death[14]. On the one hand, whether we hold with Aristotle that matter was uncreated but has a "First Mover" which explained the possibility of change or that, according to Christian Revelation, God created the heavens and the earth from nothing, in either case all that exists is in-relationship. What is more, whether we consider the remotest expression of the universe or the most fundamental particles of the atom, everything is in-relationship: atomic structure; elements; molecule; materials and so on throughout the inorganic and organic universe, permeated as it by gravity and all the other "kinds" of relationship that run throughout all that exists.

---

[13] *Gaudium et Spes*, 38 but also 36.

[14] Cf. Francis Etheredge, *The Human Person: A Bioethical Word*: https://enroutebooksandmedia.com/bioethicalword/.

On the other hand, we are, literally, conceived through relationship; both in-relationship to our parents and to God who, in the first instant of fertilization, brings the soul to exist in union with the body[15]. In other words, when a child is conceived, there is not a cell mass, a plant or any other kind of life; there is, rather, a child of the parents and of God. Thus, the human loss, whether through miscarriage or abortion, is a suffering in an existing relationship; and, therefore, death entails relationship, just as life does, in that the relationship transcends death just as a child's life transcends biological ingredients and implies the action of God[16]. Therefore, even if this is obscured by anonymous gamete donation, whether of sperm or egg, or any other kind of technological intervention that brings about a child, whether to be experimented upon or disposed of, there must be a residual sense of "being-in-relationship"; for, it is in the very being of being human to understand that life is transmitted through what men and women do or pass on – even if parenthood is never known, precisely, to them.

---

[15] As regards the union of body and soul cf. *Catechism of the Catholic Church*, CCC, 362-368.

[16] Cf. Pope St. Paul VI, *Humanae Vitae*, 13.

The Life and Death of Christ

In view of the discussion, which is to follow, on the death of Christ, particularly, it is necessary to understand the difficulty of killing a healthy human being; and, for this reason, consider the following comments by those committed to euthanasia, the deliberate killing of a human being:

'Shavelson and Parrot have identified which patients are more likely to linger, and can recommend adjustments [to the combination of drugs that are used to bring about death]. People with gastrointestinal cancer, for example, don't absorb the drugs as well. Former opiate users often have resistance to some of the drugs. Young people and athletes tend to have stronger hearts and can survive longer with low respiration rates'[17].

---

[17] "Doctors seek life-ending drugs that smooth the way for the terminally ill" by Lisa M. Krieger: https://medicalxpress.com/news/2020-09-doctors-life-ending-drugs-smooth-terminally.html; and cf. also "Is an assisted death 'quick and

Note, too, the range of people who have obviously run into the mentality that they are better off dead rather than being helped back into life!

With respect to Christ, then, He was conceived through the action of the Holy Spirit and without the help of a human father and so, although there is a difference between Christ and us[18], it is nevertheless true that He is conceived from the flesh of the Virgin Mary and, therefore, that He is of the human race and, truly, God made man (cf. Jn 1: 14). Furthermore, as He is true God and true man He is, as it were, the living intersection of all relationships: both with God and with the whole of creation. Indeed, according to the definition of person in the Councils of the Church, to be a person is "to be in-relation" and, therefore, creation is an outward expression of the inward nature of God: The Father is "in-relation to the Son and the Holy Spirit; and the Son is "in-relation" to the Father

---

painless'?" by Michael Cook: https://alexschadenberg.blog-spot.com/2021/11/is-assisted-death-quick-and-painless.html.

[18] It is not relevant to discuss the creation of Adam and Eve here; but, nevertheless, suffice it to say that they express "relationship": to God and to each other.

and the Holy Spirit; and the Holy Spirit is "in-relation" to the Father and the Son (cf. CCC, 243-256). In other words, just as all human relationships are expressly in relation to Christ (cf. *Gaudium et Spes*, 22), and He is in Himself one of the three persons of the Blessed Trinity (cf. *Gaudium et Spes*, 24), so He is in-relationship to Mary and, by implication, to everyone: to both God and man. Nevertheless, as His human life is a true human life, so His death is a true human death.

At the end of His life, the death of Christ is expressed in the departure of His Spirit: 'and bowing his head he gave up his spirit' (Jn 19: 30). Whatever the full meaning of this text is, it clearly refers to the mystery of the real death of Jesus Christ: a death verified by the soldiers who had come to make certain of it (cf. Jn 19:33). Therefore, the death of Christ was "visibly" evident and empirically verifiable. Although Christ is the Son of God and virginally conceived, the life of Christ is the life of a human being; and, therefore, His death is a rupture in the life of a human being: a kind of autumnal drop in the sap of life which, on Easter morning, "rises" again in the resurrection.

What is of particular significance for us here, however, is the moment of His death: 'and bowing his head he gave up his spirit' (Jn 19: 30). Just, then, as there was a human life from the first instant of the incarnation[19], which is the archetypal moment of all human conception[20], so His death is the moment 'he gave up his spirit' and is, accordingly, the archetypal moment of human death. Death, according to the *Gospel*, entailed giving 'up his spirit'. Now, in that moment the rootedness of the human spirit in the flesh of man is truly uprooted; and, therefore, just as the nature of His death was agonizing, so it also shows the depth of man being, as it were, 'one in body and soul' (*Gaudium et Spes*, 14). In other words, the unnaturalness of death shows through the fact that Christ's life is almost literally driven from Him in the moment of death; and, as such, this implies that human life "clings" to its bodily expression in a way that, although we cannot quite

---

[19] According to St. Thomas Aquinas the conception of Christ was immediate: 'conception of the body [does not precede] ... animation by a human soul ... in Christ', p. 484 of *Summa Theologiae*, Methuen, Pt III, Qu 5, art 5, p. 484.

[20] Fr. John Saward, drawing on St. Maximus the Confessor, says: 'Apart from the saving novelty of its virginal manner, the conception of Christ is in all respects like ours', p. *Redeemer in the Womb*, Ignatius Press: San Francisco, 1993, p. 12, but see also pp. 8-13.

comprehend it, speaks of a radical "wholeness" to human being which is, as it were, turned inside out in death.

Death, metaphysically, ruptures the wholeness of human being in that the human spirit is no longer the 'form' of the body (cf. CCC, 365), determining it to be living. Therefore, the death of Christ is a very graphic indication of the concrete relationship between body and soul: of the degree to which the spirit determines the outward expression of human life: of the spirit's profound "inherence" in the body. In other words death leaves, as it were, a "place of return" in that the dead body is ordered to the resurrection; and, metaphysically, even if the body corrupts, the totality of "human being" is retained in that it is a 'single nature' (CCC, 365): a spiritual entity ordered to its own recapitulation in the flesh in view of his or her resurrection from the dead (cf. CCC, 366).

In conclusion: Life and death are ordered to each other

If the natural life of the human body is necessarily the life of a person, then it follows that what is done to the "life" of a human being is necessarily done to the life of a person. What society permits to be done to one, by implication can be done to each one of us. Therefore, the right treatment of one person benefits us all; and where what is done is of benefit to all, then there is a multiplication of the good that can be done to each of us. What better foundation to the science of life than pondering the wondrous gift of life?!

But if, conversely, life has not departed then that life is the personal life of a human being; and, therefore, to deliberately take the life of a living man or woman, child or unborn baby, is to transgress the commandment to 'conserve life'; and, just as what is done to one implies what can be done to others, so society imperils itself as it departs from the heart of morality: 'that good is to be done and pursued and evil avoided .... so the law in us by nature commands whatever conserves human life and opposes death'[21].

---

[21] St. Thomas Aquinas, *Summa Theologiae*, translated and edited by Timothy McDermott, OP, London: Methuen, 1989, reprinted 1992; p. 287: Pt. I-II, Qu 94, art. 2.

CHAPTER SEVEN

CONVERSION IS "ANOTHER RESURRECTION"

"If today you listen to his voice, do not harden your hearts" (Hebrews 3: 15). In other words, there is a listening that lets in and there is a listening that leaves out the meaning of what is heard.

> "So that, just as Christ was resurrected from the dead through the glory of the Father, so also we too may live a new life" (Rm 6: 4). St. John Chrysostom, in the course of his commentary on Romans, says: 'Paul ... having put us in front of the future resurrection, demands from us another resurrection, a new imposition of the present life which would be the consequence of a conversion'[1].

---

[1] Second Reading, Homily, 10: 4: A reading from the "Homilies on the Letter to the Romans" of St. John Chrysostom, bishop, Cycle 2 of Ordinary Time, Week 5, pp. 259-260 of *Readings for Ordinary Time, Volume III, Weeks 1-12, Pro Manuscripto*: For private circulation only.

What follows, then, is a brief, personal account of conversion, set in the context of my life and the opening, as it were, of the transformation of life as-it-is-lived-now. But, first, an introductory look at the "the word" which makes a life-changing difference.

The word of God[2]: Grace builds on nature

At the level of psychological health, we need to share our lives to unfold who we are and to develop[3], so how much more does sharing our spiritual lives help us to develop too; and, just as opening our lives to another builds communication, so opening our spiritual lives to others opens up the possibility of communion. Thus grace

---

[2] For a more in-depth study on the Word of God, go to: Etheredge, *Scripture: A Unique Word*, Newcastle upon Tyne: Cambridge Scholars Publishing, 2014:

[3] Cf. "Chapter 7: In a Psychology Rooted in Traditional Philosophy Open to Development", pp. 125-206, of *Volume II- Faith and Reason in Dialogue*: https://www.cambridgescholars.com/product/978-1-4438-8911-7.

presupposes nature[4]. The natural desire to communicate our interior lives is transformed by grace into "confession": recognizing what God has done and is doing for me; and, therefore, sharing the recognition of what God is doing in my life[5] can give rise to the possibility, or even more, to the expectation that God will help the person listening.

In the course of this book it has been necessary to touch upon a number of "moments" in the *word of God*; indeed, those words have arisen out of listening to the word of God over some years as integral to a post-baptismal catechumenate called the *Neocatechumenal Way*: a formation in adult Christian faith[6]. Listening to the word of God, in this sense, is letting that word be itself and search the listener:

---

[4] St. Thomas Aquinas, Article 2, "Whether God's Existence Can Be Demonstrated": https://www.ccel.org/ccel/aquinas/nature_grace.vi.ii.ii.html.

[5] Cf. Chapter 14: Part I: Witness "Begets" Witness, pp. 208-220 of Francis Etheredge, *Volume III-Faith is Married Reason*: https://www.cambridgescholars.com/product/978-1-4438-9013-7.

[6] *Statute of the Neocatechumenal Way*: https://www.rmmstoronto.org/wp-content/uploads/2018/07/Statute-of-the-Neocatechumenal-Way.pdf.

'For the word of God is living and active, sharper than a two-edged sword, piercing to the division of soul and spirit, of joints and marrow, and discerning the thoughts and intentions of the heart' (Hebrews 4: 11).

And, what is more, nothing is hidden in front of this word and, as it acts, it reveals both who God is and who each one of us is:

'And before him no creature is hidden, but all are open and laid bare to the eyes of him with whom we have to do' (Hebrews 4: 12).

Thus there were three words which began, as it were, to speak to me. The first was on a World Youth Day pilgrimage to Denver, Colorado, to meet with the late, Pope St. John Paul II; and, at the time I did not know what to do with my life, having dropped out of yet more courses, given up on relationships and ever wondering about whether to be a priest or to marry – but convinced of neither and experiencing myself as estranged from others! The word which came to me was from the mass, proclaimed by the pope: "I come to give you life and life to the full" (John 10: 10). Then, a few years into having begun the Neocatechumenal Way, I was on a weekend away when the Gospel of the man thrown out threw me out: I had not changed my clothes (cf. Matthew 22: 11-14); and, showing the truth of the Lord's words, I left that meeting and returned to my sins and, like it says in the book of Proverbs: 'Like a dog that returns to his vomit is a fool that repeats his folly (26: 11).

Effort or fruit

Thus, in this final piece, I return to the beginning – not the beginning of being lonely but the new beginning of conversion; as St. John Chrysostom says: 'Paul ... having put us in front of the future resurrection, demands from us another resurrection'. On the one hand, then, what St. Paul seeks is a concrete expression of conversion: 'a consequence of ... conversion' in a change of life. In other words, that the action of God which brings about conversion is not fruitless but brings about a change of heart expressed in a change in human behaviour. One of the primary changes which God brought about was from serial relationships to marriage – from the loss of a child

to abortion because of being uncommitted[7] to eight children in marriage. But, on the other hand, this 'consequence of ... conversion' is not an invention of human effort and, indeed, if there is a pride in human effort then
there is the possibility of falling into more serious sin:

> an 'unclean spirit is sent away, but then returns and
> finds the house 'empty, swept and put in order. Then
> he goes and brings seven other spirits more evil than
> himself, and they enter and dwell there ... [Thus the
> man] becomes worse than ... [at] first' (Matthew 12:
> 44-45).

Thus, at other times, one attempt after another to
change just led from one tragedy after another including,
as I said, the pain beyond pain of discovering that a
woman had become pregnant and, calling "it" a bunch of
cells, had aborted *him or her*. We named the child and, in
due course, separated.

---

[7] Cf. "Indelible", pp. 54-56 but also pp. 49-54 of *The Prayer-ful Kiss*: https://enroutebooksandmedia.com/theprayerfulkiss/.

Conversion: A change in direction

My deference, if not reverence, for the word of God was planted without, in a sense, my realising it. Thus, although I ignored the word of God for most of my life, neither opening the Bible nor listening to it, when it came to studying it I had a definite veneration of it as a Holy Word: a word that in some sense made God present. But, at the same time as I came to study theology, which is based on the word of God (cf. *Dei Verbum*, 24[8]), I was also passing through a series of relationships; and, in a rather fitting turn of events, I failed the moral theology exam and was tempted to resign, but then resat the exam, passed and continued.

This, then, is the path that I was on and why, anyway, should I want to be going in a different direction – even an opposite direction? Because even at the level of reason I was profoundly disappointed in my relationships going nowhere, frequently ending, neither committed in marriage nor totally free because of the binding nature of coming together; and, therefore, a kind of natural

---

[8] The document of the *Second Vatican Council* on the *Word of God.*

rebellion was already surfacing even if it could go no further than recognizing, simply, that I did not want to go on
behaving in the way I did.

Consider the disciples on the way to Emmaus. They
were leaving Jerusalem, not understanding the event of
the crucifixion of Christ and He came and showed them,
through the history of salvation with which they were fa-
miliar, that His crucifixion led, in a sense, to His being
present in 'the breaking of the bread' (cf. Luke 24: 35, but
also 13-35). So, with my situation of repeated attempts to
marry indicating that there was something wrong; that
whatever I did went nowhere in terms of getting beyond
"going out" and deciding whether or not to marry. In
other words, serial relationships were not just an account
of what was happening; they were an indication of an underlying problem of being unable to marry. I somehow
knew that marriage was about "faith", whatever that was,
and I did not have the faith to marry: to decisively enter,
through the door of an unconditional vow, and to accept
the suffering entailed within it – without abandoning it.
Just as the disciples on the road to Emmaus did not understand the crucifixion of Christ and had to have Christ
explain it to them, so I did not understand the sacrament

of marriage and needed help to do so – nor could I imagine being able to live it.

The key moment, as unexpected as it was to be fruitful, was when I was considering, yet again, the frustrating fruitlessness of my life and the fact that I was unable to decide on a vocation and, in the case of marriage who, if anyone, to marry; and, therefore, as failure followed failure, what was the point of continuing and what, even, was the point of even going on living. Although, then, studying theology had its problems, such as the difficulty of grasping faith, I was still on the course and reading for an essay, when what it said in the *Catechism of the Catholic Church* spoke to me:

> 'Since God could create everything out of nothing, he can also, through the Holy Spirit, give spiritual life to sinners by creating a pure heart in them' (CCC, 298).

Conversion: "another resurrection"

Why was it that this moment was different to all other moments? Why did this word strike through to me in a way that no other word had ever done? Why was it from that moment on I went back to my *Neocatechumenal*

community, went on a pilgrimage and, after a little vacil-
lation, saw that instead of going to discern the possibility
of the priesthood that I was in fact looking for a wife?

After six months, I married a woman I knew locally,
who had also been on these pilgrimages. What decided us
that this was real and of God? One reason was the recognition that, having been asked to find work while considering the priesthood and not having done so, within a
week of discussing the possibility of marriage with my fi-
ancé and our parish priest, Fr. Tony Trafford, I was also
asked to find work and got a job working in a laundry as
a laborer. Secondly, we were both in *Neocatechumenal*
communities and were open to life. Thirdly, it was clear
that God was making a chaste courtship possible and that
everyone around us was willing to organize the wedding
and all that that entails and so we were free to go on walks
and visit people.

On the beautiful October morning of our wedding
day, the following words of the psalm ran through my
mind like a tikka tape message: "This poor man called and
the Lord heard him" (Ps. 34: 6); and, right from the beginning of our marriage, just as Christ was present at the
marriage feast of Cana, along with His mother and disciples, so we have been helped by that Gospel in which He

turned water into wine (Jn 2: 1-12), not as a one off event but as a *way of Christian marriage: turning our sufferings into joys.* So when we cannot speak, we can pray; when our resources don't seem enough, prayers are concretely answered; and so, all in all, all the suffering of having ten children in as many years is so richly rewarded that there is no comparison between the tiredness and the problems that the Lord has led us through and the good of family life that He has so generously given us. In other words, while often in the short term there are seemingly insurmountable problems, in the long term we have seen that the Lord has brought us through them. Moreover, just as His mother and His disciples were present and helpful at the marriage feast, so we have been helped by priests, the sacraments of the Catholic Church, notably the Eucharist and Reconciliation or, as it was once called, Confession, and the presence of a Christian community.

Thus, we married twenty five years ago and, in view of what faith is, believing that God exists and helps, we have ten children, two of whom were early miscarriages and, we hope, are in heaven. In other words, every child was conceived out of the hope of the help of God, especially in view of poverty, unemployment, illness and the crises of marriage. I finished my first degree and went on to do two

MAs and two more postgraduate certificates and, eventually, to work in Catholic education and then, in due course, to leave and write what are now eleven published books and numerous articles. In other words, my life is radically and concretely different from before the word of creation spoke to me[9].

Clearly, the evidence is in: God's word changed my life and began a kind of "resurrection".

---

[9] Cf. Etheredge, *The Family on Pilgrimage: God Leads Through Dead Ends*: https://enroutebooksandmedia.com/familyonpilgrimage/.

EPILOGUE

There are two, possibly three, themes to reflect upon, finally, the first is the discovery of our limitations, the second is the mystery of Christ's suffering *being for us an entrance into the significance of our own*, and the third is the praise of God which begets the beginning of eternal life!

But, first, a general note about the complementary nature of faith and reason which, directly or indirectly, has been investigated throughout this book; and, therefore, it is not about religion replacing science or science replacing religion, it is about each contributing what it can to the well-being of the whole person. Indeed, as we have seen, life entails purpose, goals, relationships, gifts as well as sufferings and, therefore, this book is about bringing all that is human to bear on all that we are going through, in order that there will be a 'fullness of life' for each and every one of us (cf. John 10: 10).

Our limitations

It is possible to consider limitations in two, if not three directions: our own limits, the limits of others, and our limitations before God.

My own limitations are expressed in beginning to understand that my life was disordered, that while I sought
and found, to some extent, a psychological understanding
of myself as a person "in search" of himself, there seemed
to be a kind of impotence in front of what I discovered.
Even, as I got older, and began to see that the sufferings I
hated so much as a child, being caned and humiliated as a
schoolboy, were themselves a symptom of an underlying
condition that had developed from even earlier and entailed stealing, lying and threatening others because I did
not want my parents to know that I was losing money
gambling. In other words, I began to realize that the sufferings that I hated so much were a sign that there was
something profoundly disordered in my life; and, even if
this did not identify its depths, it both set me on a path to
understand the origin of psychological disorders and, in
due course, took me back to original sin as an originating
cause of the imperfections in myself and in family life,
both my own and the generations which seemed to go
back, increasingly, to the beginning. Thus, little by little,
there began the beginnings of an integrated worldview
which, while it did not seek to exclude either anything rational or religious, yet seemed to be about grasping that

religious truth was a deeper and more encompassing reality than psychological thought and its explanations.

The ultimate limitation, however, was not just the limit of psychological explanations and their inability to "release" me from the chain of choices which grew out of wrongdoing – but the discovery, if it can be called a discovery, that wrongdoing had its own dynamic and kept a person prisoner, inflicting harsher and harsher sentences upon the slave to wrongdoing. In other words, and this is very difficult to communicate to others, and especially to a generation which is enamored of its technological power, there is a natural understanding of wrongdoing which arises, on reflection, from the very facts of our lives – but this is unable to establish and to deliver a renunciation of that self-same behavior.

Thus, as much as I believed in human freedom, my experience was of being a slave to my inclinations and, in time, the inclination to suicide seemed to grow out of the very "ground" of wrongdoing; and, while I pursued many types of answer to the question of what my life was about, the lasting help has come, unexpectedly, from the very Christian Faith that I had scarcely "inherited", although it had been present in my childhood. When, then, I was about fourteen and I tried to commit suicide by swallowing various pills, what entered my imagination was the possibility of being judged by Christ and the apostles and it induced a fear of God that led me to drink a lot of water and hope that I would not die; that fear of God, while not the fullness of life (cf. Jn 10: 10) which Christ promised, later, on a pilgrimage to Denver, Colorado, in my thirties, was a beginning.

The sufferings of Jesus Christ

To begin, even if, as I had, I had been brought up a Catholic, that it was scarcely possible to even think of the passion, death and resurrection of Jesus Christ; that He was, as it were, a person too remote and unconnected with the life that I lead: a barely historical figure with no personal significance. However, I do remember, vividly, looking at the face of Jesus Christ on a picture from the Shroud of Turin; the cloth that reputedly covered the body of Christ and was discovered to have a mysterious image on it that, as far as scientists can tell, does not really have an ordinary explanation. But I was not thinking of the scientific findings, about which I knew nothing at the time; rather, it was an attraction to the fact of a man who was, as it were, inexplicably present – even if it never went anywhere and, as soon as I was busy again, I would forget about Christ and His face.

At one of the worst times of loneliness when, having gone to university and begun to drop out of my courses on biological psychology, thinking that they seemed to say nothing about actual human lives, and how wrong I was to think that I could find a connection with it, and that I spent more and more time on my own, walking on beaches, going in and out of Churches, disconnected to my peers, either because going to dances was excruciatingly embarrassing or just uninteresting and boring, when unexpectedly I saw a vision of Christ crucified. Up to this point, it had seemed as if the sufferings of Christ were nothing to do with me – if I even thought of them: that it was a kind of pious reality which, in a way, had no real bearing on my life; but viewing, as it were, this image of Christ's crucifixion, it seemed as if there was a kind of unconscious sympathy between the suffering Christ and me: a common denominator of being a victim; however, this expressed a kind of moral paralysis as, indeed, being a victim implied powerlessness and an inability to act. Even though, then, there were various experiences of Christ, there was an impenetrability about them: that Christ was, like me, subject to sufferings beyond His control; but, on the other hand, was there really a connection between what He underwent and myself. Years later, even, I remember being in a church and looking at an image of His suffering as if it was an almost unintelligible act of an unmitigated torture of an innocent human being from which, indeed, I would turn my eyes – as if the contemplation of His suffering was a kind of invasion of my life. Indeed, I seem to remember being angry about it: Why was it necessary that anyone suffer like He did? What sense did it make?

So, even with a variety of "religious experiences", the death and resurrection of Christ remained, as it were, an impenetrable event; and, although absolutely central to the Christian Faith, discovering my relationship to Christ and to His death and resurrection was to take a long time and, ultimately, depended on the help of Christ coming to help with the word of the Gospels. In other words, it is not automatic that the door of Christ's suffering opens so that we begin to discover the significance of our own suffering too; indeed, it has taken many years of listening to His word and understanding that it both uncovers who we are and who He is. Nevertheless, just as Christ appeared to the disciples on the road to Emmaus (cf. Luke 24: 13-35), He can come at any time to help us enter into the significance of "our" suffering: the suffering He shares with us. But, as I have said, coming into contact with the *Neocatechumenal Way* brought me into contact with others who proclaimed, with Faith, that Christ is Lord over all our sufferings; and, therefore, that He is the one who can help us.

One particular prayer that has helped to open, little by little, the sufferings of Christ, is the Rosary: praying with Mary, the Mother of the Lord and meditating with her, as it were, on her son's life, death and resurrection. Thus there is a whole cycle of prayers, taking us through the joyful, sorrowful, glorious and now the new mysteries of light, in the life of Jesus Christ, His mother and disciples. The sorrowful mysteries begin with Christ's suffering in the Garden of Gethsemane, a particularly poignant moment of suffering alone, alone in the company of others too tired to stay awake (cf. Luke 22: 46), a suffering that begins to swell with all the moments that I, personally, have felt painfully isolated and, increasingly, it is a mystery that encompasses not just what I have been through, and still go through from time to time, but it also entails an embrace which spreads wider and wider in its capacity to encounter the sufferings that people go through in all the holes into hell that spring up and out of the tragic falls of human life.

In the end, then, whatever it is that we are going through, there is a word of life to help us; however, whether the Lord comes to us, whether anyone else helps us, it is always possible to ask God, who is always present, to help.

The contradiction of praise

This book began with the *Morning Prayer* of the Catholic Church coming to proclaim, through the psalms, that "today" is the favorable moment: that "if today we listen to His voice, let us not harden our hearts as at other times when we have disbelieved that He can help" (cf. Ps 94) – let us not declare in our hearts that there is no God or that He does not or cannot act; and, therefore, let each day, with whatever troubles it has, be a day to encounter our life, and the life of others, in the presence of the prayer of the Church, His word and the gift of hope in the help of Jesus Christ. So, whatever our daily difficulties, and this short book has ranged over many and various kinds of suffering, there is a divine help, like yeast, to raise to the fullest effect any other kind of help that may be necessary[1].

The *Morning Prayer of the Church* is made up of psalms, readings and prayers; in *The Office of Readings* for today, the 10th of March, 2022, there is a "A reading from the homilies of St. Asterius of Amasea" (Hom 13), who says: 'Look at how [Christ] ... received those who listened to his voice. He gave them a ready pardon for their sins and in a moment he quickly freed them from those who troubled them'; and then, later, he says: 'The whole story [of the lost sheep] has a sacred meaning and it warns us not to think of any man as lost or beyond hope. We must not easily despair of those who are in danger or be slow to

---

[1] Cf. Francis Etheredge, *Within Reach of You: A Book of Prose and Prayers,* St. Louis, MO: En Route Books and Media, 2021, pp. xxiv-xxv: ordering the wrong antibiotic turned out to be the right one; cf. pp. 162-167, where I share the insights which led to improving the deterioration of my legs from clots, varicose eczema etc. Finally, cf. *The Family on Pilgrimage: God Leads Through Dead Ends,* St. Louis, MO: En Route Books and Media, 2018, for a comprehensive account of how God helped the practicalities that made it possible for us to go on pilgrimage.

help them'[2]. So, while my own testimony is not of a "quick fix" and, therefore, there is no guarantee of the timescale involved in the healing of the heart, our health, and the questions of meaning, purpose and the problems of relationships which we encounter throughout our lives, the point remains that we need a sustaining hope, an enlightening word and a belief that, contrary to what we may be going through, the God who is Love is in love with us and calls us to love another (cf. 1 John 4: 7-21). Whatever, then, our own pilgrimage of life, there is a journey to be made and a gift to be obtained: that Christ comes to give us life and life to the full (John 10: 10). Therefore, without being simplistic and presuming all the difficulties of life are equal in our experience of them, nevertheless they are susceptible to the various human helps and the help of God.

So, in the spirit of life is for living and love is for loving, let us turn to the many verses of the word of God which, in their own way, go before us, invite us to find our experience addressed, and indeed anticipate a good

---

[2] *The Divine Office II: Lent and Eastertide,* Collins: London etc. 1974, pp. 110-111.

outcome; perhaps, then, beginning with this one, each of us will be guided to go further:

"God is love" (1 John: 4: 8); and, if this verse, like a net cast into the deep (cf. Luke 5: 4) dredges up problems, then we know precisely where to begin with our cry for help!

At the same time, however, let us not be naïve about the impact on our understanding of the crises of life of a materialistic understanding of the human person which, simply, contradicts the reality of the psychosomatic whole of human personhood and opens up the possibility of neglecting the most rudimentary ways that good relationships call us into life, communicate the truth about dying and recognize the reality of death.